# CAREER
# COACH

# CAREER
# COACH

## YOUR PERSONAL
## WORKBOOK FOR A
## BETTER CAREER

## Corinne Mills
Personal Career Management

*Career Coach: your personal workbook for a better career*

This first edition published in 2011 by Trotman Publishing, a division of Crimson Publishing Ltd, The Tramshed, Walcot Street, Bath BA1 5BB

© Trotman Publishing 2011

Reprinted 2014

**Author** Corinne Mills
**Designed** by Andy Prior

**British Library Cataloguing in Publication Data**
A catalogue record for this book is available from the British Library

ISBN 978 1 84455 270 2

Typeset by RefineCatch Limited, Bungay, Suffolk
Printed and bound in Malta by Gutenberg Press Ltd, Malta

To my wonderful boys: Jonathan, Elliot and Louis

# CONTENTS

Contents

# TABLE OF EXERCISES

# Table of exercises

# ABOUT THE AUTHOR

This book is entirely about you, your career journey and achieving your career objectives. However, as I'm going to be your personal career coach and guide throughout this book, let me introduce myself.

I'm Corinne Mills, Managing Director of the UK's leading career coaching and outplacement company, Personal Career Management (www.personal careermanagement.com), which I founded in 2003. In this book I'm going to share with you the career coaching techniques we've used to successfully help thousands of individuals, typically senior managers and professionals, to manage their careers. I'm proud to say that Personal Career Management has been recognised as 'the best in the business' for the quality of our career coaching by several of the UK's biggest recruitment players.

As a trained career coach, I have over 15 years' experience working in career management, I now regularly feature as the careers expert on BBC News, On the Money, The Politics Show, Daybreak and BBC Radio 2 and Radio 5Live. I also provide expert commentary and articles for the Guardian, Financial Times, Telegraph and People Management.

My first book, You're Hired! How to Write a Brilliant CV, published by Trotman in 2009, became the bestselling CV book in the UK within weeks of launch and has remained there ever since.

Before working in career management I held senior-level roles in human resources (HR), in which I was responsible for all aspects of people management including hiring and firing, staff performance and learning and development. My knowledge of how organisations really work has always been a distinct advantage when it comes to advising individuals on the job market and in-house career progression.

Like many people, I've undergone several career transitions. My early career was unconventional: until the age of 26 I worked as an actress in theatre and television and was an occasional singer in a new wave band. However, when I met my husband-to-be, I decided, like many aspiring thespians before me, that perhaps I wanted to settle down and get a 'proper' job after all.

Armed with my English and drama degree but with little experience of anything other than acting, I had countless rejections before finally landing a job as a trainee personnel officer. I worked hard and rose through the HR corporate ranks, studying at night for my MA in Human Resource Management and later becoming a Fellow of the Chartered Institute of Personnel and Development (CIPD) and chair of a CIPD branch.

As we will see in this book, most people's career decisions, including my own, are motivated by both career and personal reasons. The business decision to set up Personal Career Management was born from a belief that high-quality career coaching should be available more widely to help people manage their careers. The personal decision was due to a change in my domestic circumstances. I was on maternity leave from my job when my husband took voluntary redundancy. We'd both had hectic corporate jobs but now wanted a more family-friendly working life. Setting up business together offered us the opportunity to provide a service we passionately believed in, and to do so in a way that met our family priorities. It has been exciting, scary, fun and immensely rewarding. Eight years on we are unrecognisable from the business that started life in our front room. We have several offices, a talented coaching team and work with hundreds of clients each year throughout the UK and abroad.

My career transitions have included working freelance, being unemployed, working as an employee, being a woman returner and setting up my own business, with several changes of direction and a couple of redundancies in between. I understand what career transitions feel like from the inside and this experience has always been helpful in my coaching work.

In this book, we will be looking closely at your own career story and future direction. I am looking forward to accompanying you on that career journey, helping you understand the landscape, map your route and minimise any obstacles in your way.

Good luck,
Corinne

# FOREWORD BY JANET SHEATH

## *About career coaching*

*Career Coach* is, I believe, a truly ground-breaking career book.

For the first time, this book allows you direct access to career management techniques previously reserved for professional career consultants.

The complexity of our working lives, reconciling personal career aspirations and the demands of the current job market mean at some stage you will be facing career change, confusion or opportunities. The need to make informed choices about your career and job moves is vital.

Career coaching integrates career research and psychological theory with knowledge about the job market and organisational processes. This means that it is well placed to help you understand the world of work and your personal development. It can expand your career management capabilities, supporting you in your career transition and developing career resilience. These are core skills for 21st century career development.

I've been involved in career management for over 15 years, training and supervising over 200 UK career coaches through the master's degree course at Birkbeck. During that time I have also witnessed the evolution of Personal Career Management's career coaching model and the difference Corinne and her team of skilled, committed and experienced career coaches have made at key points in people's working lives.

Ideally we would all have access to our own personal career coach to support us at key moments when we want to make sense of where we are in our careers. Realistically this is not available to us all. This book is an inspired way to bring Corinne's tried and tested model to you direct so that you can access and work on your own career in your own time. Corinne has been able to share her many years of career coaching within the format of a user-friendly book, bringing her career management expertise and experience to a wider audience.

*Career Coach* is more than a career workbook. As important as the resources within the book, is that you will have Corinne alongside you as your own personal career coach. There is a real sense of her presence working with you as you consider your own career story and make plans for your career ahead. I hope that you too will experience the warmth, understanding and energy that Corinne offers her clients.

I wish you well on your journey together.

Janet Sheath
Teaching Fellow, Birkbeck College, University of London
Member of the Institute of Career Guidance

# ACKNOWLEDGEMENTS

Thank you, Jonathan, for your love, sense of humour and fearlessness. We make a great team

Elliot and Louis – thank you for your patience while I've been writing this book. Whatever you both grow up to be, I hope that your life and career will be fulfilling.

Thank you to Janet Sheath who has been my touchstone in my career management work. Her advice and mentoring has been invaluable and I could not have contemplated coming so far without her.

I want to say thank you to the Personal Career Management coaching team who on a day-to-day basis are helping people transform their careers. It is inspiring to work with such a talented, knowledgeable and genuinely nice group of people. Thank you also to Vicky who is so efficient at keeping the wheels turning in our head office and who helped compile the job search resources for this book.

Thank you also to the many clients I have worked with over the years. It's been hugely enjoyable and challenging and I have learnt so much from you. I have loved being able to contribute to your career transformation.

Finally, I would also like to say thank you to Beth Bishop and Alison Yates at Trotman Publishing for their support and feedback during the writing of this book.

# ABOUT THIS BOOK

Are you ready for your next career move? Have you reached the top of your career ladder and are unsure what to do next? Perhaps you are looking for a career change or a new challenge. Or maybe you've seen friends fast-track their career and want to accelerate your career too.

There may be many different reasons that have led you to read this book. These could include:

- seeking a role which will give you more responsibility, pay or development opportunities
- wanting to move from a job that you are not currently enjoying
- feeling stuck and not knowing what you want career-wise
- looking for a change in career direction or a different way of working
- wanting a better quality of life or work/life balance.

You may have been thinking about these things for a while or perhaps something has happened recently, either at work or in your personal life, which has given your career management a new sense of urgency.

Whatever your current career situation, this book is going to change your career prospects!

How is it going to do this? Well, there is no magic wand, but there is a formula. It's called personal career coaching. It will help you look objectively at your career so that you can make smart, realistic decisions regarding your next career move and turn any career aspirations from wishful thinking into reality.

I have been using career coaching for many years in my company Personal Career Management, helping thousands of individuals to successfully progress their career.

Career coaching is based on a combination of rather complicated career and psychological theory as well as practical knowledge about the job market. This has meant that until now, if you wanted career coaching, you had to go to a specialist.

However, the aim of this book is to open up a new, user-friendly route to career coaching, making it accessible for anyone who wants to pro-actively manage their career.

## *How this book works*

*Career Coach* is set out as a practical workbook with exercises at each stage of the process, taking you through a full career analysis. Throughout the book, we work towards creating your Career Action Plan, which will help make your career decisions a reality.

We will start by helping you understand your current career situation and how you got there. You will then learn how to assess your 'career capital', so that you can see what you have to offer prospective employers and how you benchmark with other candidates. You'll also get feedback on your personal strengths and workstyle from people you know, which will help you look creatively at your career options and determine the best route to achieving your career goals.

As with anything in life, the more you put in to this book, the more you will get out of it. Some exercises you will find easier than others, but every one of them is worth doing, and I recommend working through them in order, without missing any out. The exercises work best when you can immerse yourself in some deep thinking, reflection and research in a quiet, undisturbed space. There are sample answers supplied for all the exercises to guide you and these represent fairly typical types of response from our career coaching clients.

By working through the exercises, you will be able to develop your own step-by-step Career Action Plan to see you on your way to success. Many of the exercises will directly help you fill out your plan, and we have signalled where this is the case.

At the end of each part, there is a 'reflections' exercise for you to write down any ideas, key points, thoughts or questions that have emerged so far. It's a way to chart your progress in the career coaching process, capture your learning and note down anything that strikes you as significant, including actions to be taken. These will be especially important when you come to write your career summary (Part 7) at the end of the book, which will become a useful career reference document for the future.

You will find when you read the book that other people can be of enormous help in your career journey. There are particular exercises in this book for which it is suggested that you actively approach people for their input. Their feedback, advice and information can be a very effective counterpoint to your own natural subjectivity. Most people are only too happy to help if you ask them.

If you find that you need more room to write your answers than is available in this book, visit our website:

www.personalcareermanagement.com/careercoach

Here you can find selected exercises to download onto your computer. All the exercises that are downloadable are marked with the symbol ⬇.

# Understanding your current career situation

## PART 1

W e are going to start the career coaching process by conducting a very thorough career diagnosis. Your career is multi-layered and it's helpful to poke beneath the layers if you really want to understand what is going on. It's an important first stage because very often individuals focus too narrowly on what they see as their immediate career issue and make assumptions about the solutions, rather than seeing the bigger picture.

We will start by looking broadly at your current career situation and then examine it in more detail from a number of different perspectives.

## In this section we will:

✓ complete a career health check

✓ draw a picture of your world

✓ explore your work/life balance

✓ identify your priorities for change.

# 1 CAREER KICK-OFF

L et's launch the coaching process by conducting a stock-take of your current situation. As with all the exercises in this book, answer the questions as honestly as you can. There are no right or wrong answers. The exercises are simply designed to get you thinking deeply about your career.

> **TIP** Try to write as much as possible, because the act of writing can often help you articulate some unconscious thoughts which may not yet have found expression.

## Exercise 1: Career health check

1. Write your answers to the following questions, providing as much detail as you can.

2. If you are not currently working, answer the questions in relation to previous roles.

3. There's a completed example on p7 if you need a guide to what to note.

> On a Monday morning, how do you feel about the prospect of going into work?

*(Continued)*

Which aspects of your work do you like or are of interest to you?

What aspects of your work are the least enjoyable or interesting?

What have your relationships with your manager and colleagues been like?

Has your work situation affected life outside work?

When you talk about your work to others, are you positive or negative?

What do friends and family think of your career situation?

*(Continued)*

What would you like to change about your current job/career situation?

Do you know what role you would like next? If so, what is it?

Are there any threats to your current role, for example redundancy?

How employable do you think you are – and how have you tested this?

Is there anything else which is relevant career-wise?

## ✴ Example

On a Monday morning, how do you feel about the prospect of going into work?

I have a sick feeling in my stomach on the train going in. It's not so bad when I'm there, but I hate the thought of going in.

Which aspects of your work do you like or are of interest to you?

I like working with the customers, helping them find solutions to their queries and acting as an intermediary. Have good relationships with them and it feels good if I can sort out their problems for them.

What aspects of your work are the least enjoyable or interesting?

The administration work, inputting into the database, record-keeping, etc. Find it very boring. Keep getting told off by boss because they want it done in a particular way and it just feels a waste of time to be spending so much effort on it.

What have your relationships with your manager and colleagues been like?

Generally supportive but I don't think they realise just how much I do for the company on the customer side and not sure if anyone else could do that side of my job as well.

Has your work situation affected life outside work?

I don't mind talking to customers at weekends if it keeps them happy, although it can be a bit of a pain sometimes.

When you talk about your work to others, are you positive or negative?

Very negative. I do feel unappreciated and annoyed that others seem to be favourites and I am getting overlooked.

What do friends and family think of your career situation?

They think I need to get myself more organised.

What would you like to change about your current job/career situation?

A PA to do my admin.

*(Continued)*

**Do you know what role you would like next? If so, what is it?**

Want promotion within my current company or, failing that, elsewhere.

**Are there any threats to your current role, for example redundancy?**

Potential threat of redundancy.

**How employable do you think you are and how have you tested this?**

I think I am very employable but I haven't had much success with my applications for jobs.

**Is there anything else which is relevant career-wise?**

The company is restructuring at work so there is a potential threat that staff numbers may be reduced in department.

*Gary*

Now that we have completed this initial career health check and gained an overview of your current career situation, let's explore a little further and a little deeper...

# 2  YOUR WORLD

Y ou are unique
and so is your
view of the
world. Therefore the
way you see your
career is going to be
very subjective.

> Reality is merely an illusion, albeit a very persistent one.    **Albert Einstein**

For instance, you may find your job boring, while your colleague, in a similar job, loves theirs. You might find the travel into work straightforward whereas others would hate it. You may be reluctant to push yourself forward for a promotion opportunity when it arises, while a less talented peer has no such hesitation.

This subjectivity is perfectly natural and likely to be influenced by many things, including your current state of mind, your upbringing, cultural factors, self-expectations and your life experiences to date. These elements are something we shall be looking at in detail throughout this career coaching process.

There are many occasions when this subjectivity is likely to serve us well, for example helping us to endure tough times because of a belief that something better is around the corner.

However, sometimes it can place unnecessary stumbling blocks in our way. For instance, many individuals come to career coaching because they find it difficult to talk positively about themselves to others as they associate it with showing off.

In this chapter, we are going to look much more deeply at your subjective world because, whether you are aware of it or not, your perceptions about your career will be shaping your reality. They filter the information you take in and influence your behaviour and career decisions. Where emotion is involved, your perceptions may be skewed even further than usual.

So to help you understand your inner landscape a little more, complete the following exercise to go deeper into your world.

# Exercise 2: Picture your world

**2**

1.  You are going to draw a picture of your world. It is not meant to be a realistic picture but a personal one: your drawing ability is the least important part of this exercise. You might want to use colour to make it come alive and boost your creativity.

2.  Your drawing could be lifelike, abstract or in the form of a diagram. It could include physical things such as people or places as well as more intangible elements such as emotions, events or metaphors.

3.  There are no rules about what you should put in your drawing, but some suggestions might include:
    *   your key challenges, for example difficult relationships at work
    *   any issues you feel you are wrestling with, like career indecision or inner conflicts
    *   significant people, including family members and loved ones
    *   your health and well-being, for example stress or anxiety
    *   your commitments and priorities, such as family life and hobbies
    *   your social life and activities outside work.

> **TIP** Find a way to represent in your picture any emotions you feel.

4.  Be as spontaneous as possible and include anything that comes into your head – even if it seems relatively minor in the scheme of things. Enjoy being creative and expressive. You are the only one who needs to understand your picture, so don't worry about how it looks.

5.  Take a minimum of 20 minutes to do your drawing, which you can either complete below or on a separate piece of paper which you should keep for reference.

**6.** There is an example on p13 that you can use for inspiration.

**7.** Once you have finished your drawing, take a moment to look at the whole picture and think about what it is telling you. Now answer the questions below.

What key elements did you choose to include in your picture and why?

Are there people in your picture? If so, describe the nature of your relationship with them.

What, if any, emotion(s) did you feel or represent in the picture? For example love, pride, uncertainty, frustration.

Did your picture show any areas of conflict or tension?

What are the positive aspects of your picture?

Are there any important elements missing from the picture that you have forgotten or perhaps taken for granted?

What do you see as your current challenge?

*(Continued)*

If you could choose to change just one element of your current situation, what would it be?

Is there anything you could do right now that would change your picture for the better?

Did anything else come out of this exercise for you?

**✷ Example**

My World Picture

**What key elements did you choose to include in your picture and why?**

Me running around all over the place because it feels like I am always in a rush. Included image of me gardening because I feel that things that I enjoy and need to do at home are neglected because I don't have time. Love doing the bedtime stories with the kids but am often half asleep so not giving them the attention they deserve.

**Are there people in your picture? If so, describe the nature of your relationship with them.**

Kids and grandparents are in the picture. If it weren't for the grandparents, my job wouldn't be possible so am very dependent on them but this can bring its own difficulties. Kids are good but I feel guilty that sometimes I just feel too tired to give them the attention they want.

**What, if any, emotion(s) did you feel or represent in the picture? For example love, pride, uncertainty, frustration.**

Exhaustion seemed to be the main emotion I felt. Feeling tired from running around everywhere. Felt guilty about the kids and frustrated by my mum who is really good at looking after the kids after school but is often quite critical of me and can be insensitive.

**Did your picture show any areas of conflict or tension?**

The stress of always rushing across town to be somewhere – always worried about being late. Difficult relationship with my mum but feels like everything would fall apart if I didn't have her to rely on. Never feeling like I have any personal down-time.

**What are the positive aspects of your picture?**

The kids are good. The fact that I do have my mum to help. The fact that I have a job.

**Are there any important elements missing from the picture that you have forgotten or perhaps taken for granted?**

My ex-partner – noticeable by their absence. Haven't included any friends or social life but perhaps that is because it feels non-existent at the moment. Although friends have been a great source of support to me.

**What do you see as your current challenge?**

Reclaiming my life – while protecting my income. Seems too risky to make a job move but cannot continue as I am because I will 'burn out'.

*(Continued)*

**If you could choose to change just one element of your current situation, what would it be?**

To be able to work more flexibly, ideally from home a couple of days a week, would be great.

**Is there anything you could do right now that would change your picture for the better?**

Talk to my boss about more flexible working. Look for a new job that could offer this.

**Did anything else come out of this exercise for you?**

I feel cornered. I know what I should do but it requires more energy than I have at the moment and that is making me feel very frustrated both at myself and my circumstances.

*Andrea*

How did you find this exercise? Did you get really involved in drawing the picture? Were you able to express how you feel about things right now? If you didn't, try the exercise again, this time giving yourself permission to really engage with it. You need to do this with all the exercises in this book to get maximum benefit.

# Viewing your world

Let's look more closely at what you've drawn, and why.

These pictures often express very clearly where the problems or tensions lie in our current situation, how strongly we feel about them and how they relate to other aspects of our lives.

For instance, I've seen many pictures where the drawer has been feeling uncertain of their career and this has dominated almost the whole picture, represented by big question marks, black clouds or crossroads that dwarf everything else in comparison. Other pictures represent the tug of war that is work/life balance, showing the individual physically stretched on both sides; or a central idea around which everything else orbits, such as the family, religion, money, a career goal.

If elements of your picture seem disproportionately large, this may reflect just how much time you are spending thinking, worrying or dealing with

> I was standing in treacle – stuck, weighted down, messy. Whereas everyone else around me was whizzing around. Everyone else seemed to be fine but I felt unimportant, stuck, ignored. **David**

them. I remember a client's picture that had a huge vacuum cleaner as the central symbol, representing the individual's feeling of being overwhelmed by the challenge of holding down a job and trying to keep the house in order. Hoovering wasn't the most important thing in her life – but what it represented for her was very powerful indeed.

Because your picture is a subjective one, interpreting your picture is very personal. Only you really know why you chose to include some items and not others and why you represented them in the way you have. This exercise is simply a reflection of some of the conscious and subconscious thoughts that feel very intense for you right now.

Understanding your emotional landscape is an essential part of the career coaching process because managing your career can be very challenging psychologically. It often involves activities outside most people's normal comfort zones, such as having to sell your skills to a prospective employer. Your emotions can be a great motivator to propel you into action but they can also sometimes make things more difficult than they need to be.

This exercise was designed to raise awareness of your emotional forces at work. You may find that these pop up repeatedly as you continue your career coaching journey

> My picture reflected back to me how little confidence I had in my own abilities. It was full of self-doubt – even though I had had a really good appraisal this year. I didn't include any of the people who were supportive to me and just focused on the negative people. **Angela**

through this book. If you are aware of their influence, you can decide whether you want them to exercise their power over you or not.

Later in the book, in Chapter 20, we will be looking specifically at the practical strategies you can use to manage your emotions during a period of career transition and challenge any personal perspectives that may be preventing your progress.

# 3  WORK/LIFE BALANCE

Now we are going to move to another vantage point from which to view your current situation – your life outside working hours.

Work/life balance may be the reason you picked up this book and the thing you most want to change about your career. However, even if it's not something that particularly bothers you, it's still worth working through this chapter. It will give you a useful benchmark for a happy and healthy work/life balance, something that always needs careful monitoring.

## *Getting the balance right*

While many employers have adopted more flexible, family-friendly policies, encouraged by legislation, there is still a strong expectation that when you are at work your personal life doesn't intrude into work time.

However, in the career coaching process, it is important to move away from the forced compartmentalisation of your working and personal life. Even if you think you can keep them separate, the reality is that they are in constant dialogue.

You may have career ambitions but you are likely to have life aspirations too. These may be about having a loving relationship, travelling the world, moving house, raising happy children, making a difference to the world, deepening your spirituality or anything else that is fundamental to your sense of self and life's purpose. These are likely to influence your career choices too.·

> It was when I realised I only had suits for work and jogging bottoms for around the house that it hit me that I never do anything outside of work.    **Karen**

You will also have other roles, responsibilities and interests, for example as a parent, partner, friend, carer, citizen, contributing towards your community or pursuing hobbies and causes close to your heart.

Ideally, your career will work in as complementary a way as possible to your personal life. However, there are often tensions.

> If you neglect to recharge a battery, it dies.    **Oprah Winfrey**

Some of these may even have been revealed in Exercise 2. Sometimes these tensions require relatively minor or temporary compromises which we feel we can live with. You may need to occasionally work late to complete a project, meet a tough deadline or deal with an emergency. Your job may involve frequent travelling or weekend work, but if you and your family are happy to accept this, it isn't necessarily problematic.

However, work/life balance does need careful monitoring because it is very easy for work to become all-consuming, leaving little time and energy for anything else. If we don't make time for other activities and interests outside work, then we can become dangerously insular and lose our sense of personal identity. Everyone needs a 'hinterland' of other interests to help us keep perspective and remind us that we are human and not a work machine. Otherwise we can place a real strain on our health, well-being and relationships and that is not good either for our career or our personal life.

This is not to say that we shouldn't work hard because if we want to progress our career, or even stay in our job, that is what we are expected to do. There is also no doubt that in times of economic uncertainty, there are additional pressures on workloads because of staff redundancies.

# *Thinking about your balance*

The reality is that many individuals not only work long hours but are also constantly thinking about work, to the possible detriment of their personal life.

Does this sound like you? Perhaps not. But if you are someone whose exhaustive commitment to your job means that you collapse when you get home, leaving little time or energy for anything else, is this because of the expectations of your company? Are you working late because there is a genuine need? Or could it be that you, rather than your employer, are responsible for blurring the work/life boundary?

> Forty per cent of employees say they are under excessive pressure at work, either every day or once or twice a week, with increases in the proportion of public sector and voluntary sector staff reporting excessive pressure. Only 58% of employees felt that they achieved the right balance between their work and home. *CIPD Employee Outlook Report, Winter 2010–2011*

Work/life imbalance is a very common problem that individuals bring to career coaching. Sometimes the solution is just to find another job, or on occasion another profession. For instance if you work in investment banking you have to expect early starts and working late into the evening.

> I had a difficult customer who would regularly ring me at weekends just to whinge. It would wind me up terribly. Then one day I'd just had enough and told her that I wouldn't be available to take her calls at the weekend. She still tried it, but I let it go to voicemail. She is still pretty unpleasant but at least I only have to put up with her during the week now. I should have laid down the ground rules with her at the start. *Sian*

However, it can equally be the individual's self-expectations that are causing the problems.

My boss is sending me emails at all times of the day and night. Do I have to become a workaholic insomniac too? **Paul**

I've worked with several clients who came to career coaching in a desperate state because they felt their employer was expecting them to work all hours. One example included a female manager who felt 'burnt out'. She would work late and come in very early in the morning in order to clear the backlog. Did her organisation really require her to work all these hours? No, they didn't. Would it have been acceptable to have some backlog? Yes. Unless they were going to employ an additional person, some backlog would be inevitable. Had she ever raised this as an issue with her employer? No. It transpired that there had been a similar pattern in her last three jobs. Her work/life imbalance was more to do with her low self-esteem and lack of assertiveness than a hard taskmaster of an employer. She would take the problem with her to every job unless she learned how to redraw her own work/life boundaries.

According to statistics from the Health and Safety Executive, during 2009–2010, 1.3 million people suffered from an illness they believed was caused or made worse by their current or past work.

This is not to say that unreasonable bosses don't exist, nor organisations with a culture of long working hours, because of course they do.

But if you are someone who continually works long hours, there is a cost. Your personal life is not the only thing that will suffer; your work performance will too. Tiredness can impair your judgement and cognitive abilities so that you start making mistakes and the quality of your work will deteriorate. You are also much more likely to fall ill.

It may be far better to finish off work at a reasonable time and then attack the work with gusto the next morning when you are feeling rested. If the workload is really unmanageable it is also worth talking to your manager. Ask them to decide which of your tasks are priorities and which can wait. Request an extended deadline or additional support. Unless you tell them there is a problem, they won't know until you fail to deliver, and that's never the best time to be having a conversation with your manager.

# Improving the balance

Most people find it tricky to some extent to balance their work and personal life, but there are lots of things that you can do to improve your work/life balance.

The following exercise will help flush out any work/life conflicts that need addressing and provide some suggestions for how you can improve your work/life balance.

# Exercise 3: Work/life balance assessment

1.  Consider the different personal aspects of your life as outlined in the headings below including:
    - What is working well?
    - What impact, if any, does it have on your working life or vice versa?
    - What needs improvement and how could you bring this about?

2.  Write your answers in the box on p23. Add any other headings if there are other aspects of your life you feel need attention.

3.  You'll find an example on pp24–25.

## ✻ Family

Do you feel that you have quality time with the family? This might include having fun weekends together, being able to help the kids with their homework, caring for an aged parent or simply visiting family members.

## ✻ Personal relationships

On the romantic front, are things as you would wish them to be? Are there other significant relationships that are not working as you hoped they would?

## ✻ Finances

Everyone would like more money, but do you have financial problems? If so, what are the risks and what do you need to do about the situation?

## ✵ Fun

What is your social life like? Do you have sufficient down-time outside work? Do you have fun times when you can just enjoy yourself and recharge your batteries?

## ✵ Personal growth

Are you as intellectually, spiritually or even physically stretched as you would wish to be? Are you interested in learning and development, self-help literature or the arts? Do you follow a faith? Do you enjoy physical challenges like training for marathons or learning to dance?

## ✵ Community

Do you have community responsibilities that are important to you? For instance, volunteering for a charity, supporting a political party, sitting on the PTA or residents' association. Are you as involved in your community as you would like to be?

## ✵ Health and well-being

Have you any health concerns? Do you feel good about yourself? Are there concerns about the health and well-being of any of the people who are close to you?

## ✵ Other personal needs

Is there anything else going on in your life that is causing tensions or needs attention?

Family

Personal relationships

Finances

Fun

Personal growth

Community

Health and well-being

Other personal needs

## ✳ Example

### Family

Kids are doing fine at school. Wife is enjoying her new job. Mum is going to need more help in the future. Work have been understanding about mum but it does take time looking after her.

### Personal relationships

Happily married. Don't go out much. When I work late it does cause arguments because we both get ratty. Should start to minimise late working at the office and start to go out more at the weekend and even maybe mid-week go for a drink together or to the cinema.

### Finances

I have a job so income coming in but having to dig into savings. No pay rise at work for two years yet everything going up in price. Need to do something to increase income. Ask boss for a pay rise? I need a better-paid job, but should I also look to reduce outgoings?

### Fun

When we go out we do have a good time together. Weekends often spent on routine stuff – not enough fun. Work can be very stressful so need to let off some steam at weekends and chill out otherwise work would feel just overwhelming. Should start inviting friends over. Organise some weekend breaks.

### Personal growth

Really enjoyed my management course. Learned a lot. Feel I've got lots more to learn. I'm using the knowledge in current role but definitely good for the next step up. I should find the time to read more books on leadership and see if more courses available. Talk to HR about what they would recommend.

### Community

Got involved with the Fun Run which was good. Feel bad that I am not doing anything with the kids' schools. There are initiatives at work to encourage employees to get involved with their local communities but I haven't really done anything about that yet. Could help out with the Scouts when they need 'dad' help.

*(Continued)*

### Health and well-being

Lost half a stone in weight with recent flu. Do feel very stressed. Seem to have constant colds and flu so not 100%. Need to go back to gym – maybe have a health check and watch the wine intake.

### Other personal needs

Want to help my son prepare for his exams as I know he is struggling a bit. Maybe I should do an MBA. Would love to travel to China.

*Stephen*

Let's identify some practical actions you can take which will improve the work/life balance issues you have pinpointed. To help you I have included some suggestions below, but add as many others as you can that are relevant for you.

## ✳ *Reclaiming your work/life balance*

Tick if you want to action this

### At work

| | |
|---|---|
| Leave work on time | ☐ |
| Reclaim lunch hours and take sensible breaks | ☐ |
| Resist checking emails at weekends | ☐ |
| Ask to work flexible hours | ☐ |
| Avoid rush-hour traffic | ☐ |
| Set realistic work deadlines | ☐ |
| Delegate where you can | ☐ |
| Say no to unreasonable requests | ☐ |
| Create 'do not disturb' times at work | ☐ |
| Manage demanding people more effectively | ☐ |
| Talk to your boss about any work/life issues | ☐ |
| Work more efficiently | ☐ |
| Write a to-do list with priorities for the day | ☐ |
| Set realistic goals for yourself and others | ☐ |
| Take all your annual leave! | ☐ |

### At home

Incentivise the kids to do household chores

Try internet shopping

Get a cleaner, au pair, etc. for chores

Go to bed earlier/get up earlier

Reduce clutter

Reduce your commitments outside work

### Family and personal relationships

Make time for romance

Visit extended family

Play with the kids

Invite friends round

Avoid or tackle toxic relationships

Arrange respite care if you have caring responsibilities

Prioritise school plays and other important events

Arrange Skype video calls when you are travelling

### Fun

Start a social diary to plan your 'fun'

Arrange a babysitter

Organise a weekend away

Join a sports team

Enrol on an evening course

Have a holiday with friends

Go out to dinner or the pub after work

Meet up with old friends on Facebook

Throw a party

### Finances

Get financial advice

Set a budget and stick to it

Cut spending so you can reduce your hours

Ask for a pay rise

If self-employed, increase your rates

### Personal growth

Go to church, temple or mosque

Read books

Take up yoga

Go on a self-help course ☐
See a counsellor ☐
Embark on a physical challenge such as climbing a mountain ☐
Go travelling ☐
Learn a language ☐
Trace your ancestors ☐

## Community

Do some voluntary work ☐
Be a mentor ☐
Help at the school ☐
Join a local committee ☐
Help a neighbour ☐
Join a charity group ☐
Fight for a cause ☐

## Health and well-being

Get a health check ☐
Eat healthily ☐
Take up a hobby ☐
Go for walks ☐

## Any other suggestions

☐
☐
☐
☐
☐

---

**TIP** This exercise will help you fill out your Career Action Plan on p227. If improving work/life balance is something that is especially important for you, revisit this exercise when you compile your plan in Chapter 22.

---

Even at this early stage in the career coaching process, you should be able to see that there are changes you can make which can make a difference to your career – and to your life.

# 4  AN OBJECTIVE ASSESSMENT

So far we have looked at your career from a number of different perspectives. We have taken an initial career health check and explored both your inner landscape and your life outside work. The aim so far has been to give you the opportunity to express your emotions, frustrations, conflicts and concerns in a structured way. They are important, they matter to you and the exercises we have done so far are a way for you to articulate the career issues that drive or trouble you.

However, as human beings we often tend to focus on all the things that are wrong about a given situation and ignore some of the good things. Looking back on the exercises we have done, you may notice this in your answers. Are they more negative than you were expecting?

## *Don't jump to conclusions*

When individuals are in an uncomfortable career situation, their emotions can make their thinking one-sided and it can be more difficult for them to see what is in their best interests.

For instance, I speak to many individuals who tell me they want to hand their notice in, even though they haven't another job to go to.

They haven't considered that it can take time to find another role; that unemployment is very stressful; and that it is often easier to find another job while you are still working. It's important to take all this into account when making the decision to resign, and not act purely on emotion.

Equally, I talk to many people who assume, sometimes wrongly, that the only way to develop their career is to leave their current job. They find it easier to move to a new company than have an honest conversation with their manager about internal career opportunities.

> I liked my organisation but just felt like I was treading water so I started applying externally for jobs and got a job offer. When I told my boss I was handing my notice in they said they would be really sorry to lose me and what would make me stay? I said that I had been frustrated that I hadn't been more involved in strategy. The next day they came back and offered for me to become part of the strategy team which was just fantastic. I wished I had talked to them earlier and saved myself time and anguish. **Katherine**

In fact, if you do a good job for your organisation, they are likely to want to keep you and so may be willing to find ways to help you in your career progression. But unless you ask, you will never know. It makes sense to at least make sure you are aware of any internal options before you decide to go.

This final chapter in Part 1 is designed to help you take a more dispassionate view of your current career situation and examine both the positive and the negative aspects equally.

---

**TIP** Don't be afraid to ask at work about opportunities for career development. It will show your motivation and commitment to self-improvement, which is good for both you and the organisation.

---

# Exercise 4: Values questionnaire

This exercise will help you think about the things that are important to you in your career and assess to what extent these are currently being met. It will help raise your awareness about where there are gaps as well as any things you may be taking for granted.

1.  Tick the 10 work values in the list below that are the most important to you.

2.  Rank them in importance with 10 being the most important and 1 the least important. Feel free to add any others you feel are relevant for you.

3.  From your top 10 list, tick those that are currently being met and those that are not.

> **TIP** If you are not working at the moment, you may wish to complete this with reference to a previous job or jobs.

| Value | Ranking 1–10 (10 = most important) | Currently being met Y/N |
|---|---|---|
| To succeed as a result of your own capabilities | | |
| To be well liked by others at work | | |
| To have autonomy and define your own priorities and schedules | | |
| To be challenged and have new problems to solve | | |
| To work in a role that supports your personal life | | |
| To have power and influence | | |
| To be a catalyst for change | | |
| To have social contact with others | | |
| To use creativity and self-expression | | |

*(Continued)*

| | | |
|---|---|---|
| To be recognised as an expert | | |
| To achieve personal development and growth | | |
| To help improve individual, social and/or political well-being | | |
| To make a difference to the team/organisation | | |
| To work and live where you want | | |
| To earn as much money as possible | | |
| To increase your career seniority and status | | |
| To participate in decision-making | | |
| To be appreciated for your efforts | | |
| To identify with the cause/product of the organisation | | |
| To be able to travel | | |
| To use physical skills and abilities | | |
| To become well known in your field | | |
| To work in accordance with personal, spiritual or ethical ideals | | |
| To work in a role compatible with health and fitness aims | | |
| To have intellectual challenge | | |
| To pursue knowledge | | |
| To have social status as a result of your job | | |
| To work with stimulating people | | |
| To have security and predictability | | |
| To take risks | | |
| To have variety and change | | |
| Other values: | | |
| | | |

4. Write down below which of your values are being met and which aren't. Why? Remember to focus on the positives as well as the negatives.

| Values being met | Values not being met |
|---|---|
| | |

## ⭐ *Example*

| Values being met | Values not being met |
|---|---|
| I am paid relatively well for what I do so I am able to enjoy a comfortable lifestyle. | Not able to use my creativity and self-expression: I've felt very stifled in previous roles. I am a creative person and I think I can bring a fresh approach and new ideas but the organisations I've worked for have been very rigid. |
| I have social status because others see my role as very interesting and want to talk about it. I like this but it isn't really as glamorous as other people think it is. | Developed ideas but don't feel they were given proper consideration. Stopped even trying. I want to work in an environment where ideas are welcomed. |
| I like the travel aspects of my job. | *Graham* |

From this exercise you should be able to see that, even if the job you are in currently is not perfect, there are likely to be some values that are being met and some elements about it which are positive (for example, you might work close to home).

Let's continue to look at both the good and the bad aspects of your current career situation. The aim is for you to be able to see both sides of the coin. For the following exercise, put on your rational, analytical hat again and set your emotions to one side.

## Exercise 5: Career positives and negatives

**5**

1.  Write down as many positive things as you can about your current career situation, for example the fact that your company has a good pension scheme.

2.  Write down as many negative things as you can about your current career situation, for example a threat of redundancy or lack of opportunities.

3.  Make the lists as balanced as you can – have an equal number of items on each side.

> **TIP** You might find it helpful to ask someone else to play 'devil's advocate' with you if one side is more heavily weighted than the other.

| Positives | Negatives |
| --- | --- |
| | |

## ⚘ Example

| Positives | Negatives |
|---|---|
| Good access to training. | Threat of redundancy. |
| Might be opportunities with the new restructuring. | Staff cuts will mean more work. |
| Some flexibility about working hours. | Don't know how service will continue with less staff. |
| Like working in this industry. | Will have to compete with colleagues. |
| Pension benefits. | Pay freeze. |
| | *Gillian* |

I am very comfortable in my current job. It's close to home, relatively secure and although the pay isn't great, it's steady. However, looking at the negatives, it made me realise that I am in danger of becoming de-skilled as I am not doing half of the things I am capable of or learning anything new. I think that could make me very vulnerable if I had to find another job.

*Rashid*

Did you find it easy to fill in both the positive and the negative columns? Or was it far easier to do one side than the other?

When people feel strongly about something – and they usually do when they are dissatisfied with elements in their career – they will be biased. They will then often look for evidence to support that view. Make sure you have acted on point 3 of the exercise, and have tried to make your list as balanced as possible.

The useful thing about this exercise is that it forces you to consider both perspectives and challenge your own assumptions. You may still make the same decisions you would do before thinking about it, but at least you have fully considered the counter-argument.

## Identifying positive changes to make

Now that we have completed a full career diagnostic of your current situation, let's determine what the positive changes are that you want to bring about in your career.

# Exercise 6: I want ...

**6**

1. Review all the exercises in Part 1 of this book to capture all the things that you want to be different and then complete the following 'I want ...' sentences.

2. You may want to include:
   - things you want to be different, for example 'I want to be paid more'
   - things you want to be the same, for example 'I want to carry on working part time'
   - emotional wants and needs, for example 'I want to rediscover my motivation'
   - areas of uncertainty that you want to resolve, for example 'I want to understand my career options.'

Do not censor or edit this list. Write down everything that is important to you.

> **TIP** You are allowed to be demanding in this exercise. Write down everything you want to be different. These can be practical or emotional. Include them all.

I want ...

I want ...

I want ...

I want ...

*(Continued)*

I want ...

I want ...

I want ...

I want ...

## ✳ Example

I want ... to feel that I have made a difference to the world.

I want ... to make good use of my time.

I want ... to work with people who are passionate about the cause.

I want ... to work with an organisation that has power.

I want ... to safeguard my earnings.

I want ... to know whether I should stay or find a new job.

*Michael*

In the above exercise you will have identified your career needs and wants for the future. Bear these in mind as you work through the rest of this book.

They will be important touchstones when we come to look at your options for the future in Part 5.

# The reality of your situation

As we have seen throughout Part 1, your career situation is unique, complex and multi-faceted. Whatever your circumstances, you should now have a deeper insight into and some fresh perspectives on your current career situation.

In the reflections exercise below, record any challenges you feel you are facing, whether they are of a practical or more emotional nature. If you can express them and articulate them, the chances are you can do something practical about them.

# Exercise 7: Reflecting on Part 1

Review the following exercises:

- Exercise 1: Career Health Check (p3)
- Exercise 2. Picture of your world (p9)
- Exercise 3: Work/life balance assessment (p21)
- Exercise 4: Values questionnaire (p30)
- Exercise 5: Career positives and negatives (p33)
- Exercise 6: I want … (p35)

1. What have you found particularly helpful in these exercises?
2. Are there any themes, words or phrases that seem very appropriate or keep popping up?
3. What emotions have you felt, or haven't you felt; and why you think you responded in that way?
4. Are there any actions you can take that will make a difference?

---

**TIP** Look out for any recurring words or phrases that you are using. Consider why those words seem so appropriate for you.

## ✳ *My reflections on where I am now*

> **TIP** We will revisit this reflections exercise again when we look back on your career coaching journey in exercise 48, p250.

## ✳ *Action points*

## ✳ *Example: my reflections on where I am now*

The exercises in this section really hit home for me that I'm spending all my time working and not enough time having fun. I need to work harder at my social life. I get so focused on my career to the exclusion of everything else – and it's not good for me. The relationship part has definitely suffered and I need to invest some time in this.

Because I've had to take over the role of a colleague who has been made redundant, I'm feeling quite stressed because of the increased workload. Have been getting migraines – and been grumpy with my partner because it's really been getting to me. I don't want to fail – because I don't want to be made redundant, but the more stressed I get, the less capable I feel.

I probably need to discuss with my manager what her priorities are rather than trying to do everything at once, which is unachievable. She has just kind of left me to it, but I think I need to understand her priorities and then I can choose where to direct my energies rather than trying to do everything all at the same time. If that doesn't help, I think I need to look for another job.

I think my migraines will probably reduce if I'm less stressed and also remember to eat regularly rather than skipping meals because I'm too busy. I know family life will improve if I'm less stressed.

*Liz*

## ✳ *Example: action points*

1. Make an appointment to discuss priorities with my manager.
2. Start job-searching.
3. Take lunch breaks and eat properly.

In Part 1, we have looked in detail at your current situation from both a career and a personal perspective and identified your priorities for change.

However, you haven't just magically arrived at this point in time. You have a long and interesting history that has brought you here, comprising important events, key decisions and formative experiences.

# How you got here

Understanding your past enables you to put your current situation in context. Your past patterns of behaviour can also be a useful predictor of the type of career challenges that are likely to prove trickiest for you in the future, as well as those you are more likely to sail through. The more you can anticipate potential difficulties, the better you can equip yourself with the resources you need to overcome them.

So in Part 2, we are going to look at the obstacles you have faced in the past; the coping strategies you used; the things that worked for you and those that didn't; and the key influences which shaped your personal and career development.

**In this section we will:**

✓ look at your key life events

✓ create your autobiography

✓ discover the key influences that have shaped your personal history

✓ document your work history in detail.

# 5 YOUR PERSONAL HISTORY

I n your past there will have been a number of turning points where you made particular career decisions. Some of those decisions may have been well thought out, while others may have been more spontaneous or even forced upon you.

How far has your career to date been planned? Have there been times when your career seemed to be progressing well and

> I had to look after my mum from an early age as she was very ill. Becoming a nurse was a natural extension of looking after my mum.
> **Mary**

other times when you were completely miserable at work? We are going to look at how you have dealt with those different scenarios.

Alongside your career, you are likely to have also had peaks and troughs in your life. Most people will have had to face, at some time or other, difficult circumstances such as unemployment, ill

> Work was so stressful that I got really ill so I quit my job, went travelling and came back in a much better state of mind. Found myself a more junior job with less pressure. I'm so much happier.
> **Ed**

health, relationship breakdowns, financial difficulties or the loss of a loved one. These can be extremely stressful and their effects can be felt for a long time afterwards. Have any of these difficulties influenced your career journey to date and if so, what impact did they have or, indeed, continue to have?

Try to approach the following exercises with a rational and analytical approach as though you are a historian sifting through the evidence or a biographer commissioned to profile an important figure.

Be your own biographer – warts and all! Let's hear your story.

You may find that some of these exercises arouse some surprisingly powerful emotions, especially if they touch on particularly sensitive areas. If this happens you might either find it wonderfully cathartic or perhaps unsettling. Be aware of your own limits and go only as deeply into these exercises as you feel comfortable with. The aim is not to make you miserable, so if it feels too raw or unsettling, back away.

> **TIP** These exercises are very personal, so stay within your comfort zone when contemplating any deeply sensitive areas.

Let's start by looking at the most significant events that have happened to you in your life to date.

**8**

## Exercise 8: My life events ⬇

1. On the diagram opposite or on a separate sheet of paper, plot the key moments and events in your life to date, starting from birth on the left side of the line until the current date. Examples could include:
   - educational history and achievements
   - your job history
   - happy events, for example falling in love or winning a competition
   - traumatic events, for example accidents, illness or a bereavement
   - adventures, for example travelling
   - achievements, for example awards or recognition
   - challenges, for example redundancy, relationship breakdown
   - other significant events, for example building your own house, raising money for charity.

2. For each event, place an X on the chart to indicate how positive or otherwise you felt about each experience or event shown on the chart (refer to the example on p47 to help you).

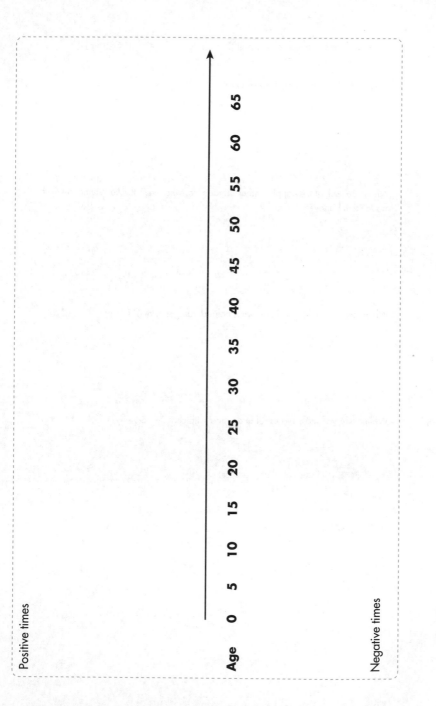

**3.** Now answer these questions to help you debrief this exercise.

What did it feel like doing this exercise?

When you look at the happiest times in your life, what were the key elements which made them happy?

When there were difficult times, what helped you get through?

When were you most successful at dealing with change and why?

Write down three key points that emerge for you from this exercise:
1.
2.
3.

*Example*

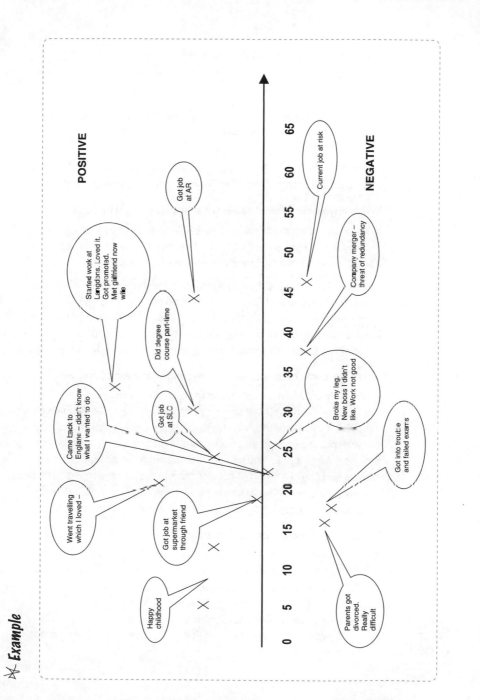

**What did it feel like doing this exercise?**

*Okay. But surprised how much it still rankles that I didn't do as well as I should have in my school exams.*

**When you look at the happiest times in your life, what were the key elements which made them happy?**

*Loved my role at Langdons. Think this was because there was a real team spirit and it felt like we were doing stuff that mattered. Met my wife around same time. Both work and personal life were great.*

**When there were difficult times, what helped you get through?**

*It was horrible when I came back to England and I kept getting rejected for jobs I knew I could do. But I just had to get on with it so kept applying and eventually heard about the job at SLC from a friend.*

*When I broke my leg I had a new boss whose first experience of me was being off on sick leave. The relationship was never a good one. Decided to take a degree as wanted to prove to the boss that I was capable. Knew I had to take my career development in my own hands because my boss would not help me. Felt great handing in my notice when I got my new job.*

**When were you most successful at dealing with change and why?**

*It was difficult when Langdons got taken over as they wanted to do things differently. I did tell them when I thought they were making mistakes but also said when I thought their ideas were better. Think they respected my openness and that I wasn't just being awkward for the sake of it. I also helped persuade others to accept difficult change and I think that this bought me a lot of credibility with the new manager. As a result I still had a job while many of my colleagues left or were made redundant. Wife was very supportive throughout.*

**Write down three key points that emerge for you from this exercise.**

1. *I'm probably more resilient than I thought, have been through some difficult times but have been quite determined to get what I want*
2. *Bit of a hang-up about my school education – feel like I'm not as good academically as others. However, getting my degree helped.*
3. *Relationships at work have been as important as the job itself – particularly my relationship with my manager. The wife is a great sounding board.*

*James*

This exercise charts the key points in your career and life history. While it is interesting to look back on significant events, it is the way you have *responded* to these circumstances that is of particular interest in terms of your career coaching.

> It was really hard when my marriage broke up. I was very low. Work proved a useful distraction, kept me busy and helped preserve the little of what was left of my self-esteem.
> **Rachel**

Do you think that other people might have responded to those events in a similar way? How would people who were close to you at the time have described the way you dealt with difficult challenges?

# Exercise 9: Your autobiography

This autobiographical exercise takes us beyond life events to look at some of the other formative influences and experiences that have helped shape your story and your career to date.

1. Write your autobiography, focusing in particular on stories and experiences that you consider helped shape the person you are today. You may find this easier to write on a separate piece of paper or as a downloadable document on your computer.

2. Write it with yourself in mind as the intended audience. It's up to you whether you want to show it to anyone else.

3. Feel free to write as much as you wish. You can write it in a very structured chronological way or be more free-flowing. You might find it easier to break down your autobiography into seven-year chunks, for example ages 0–7, 7–14, 14–21 and so on, as we did in Exercise 8.

4. You might include:
   - earliest memories
   - family experiences
   - educational experiences at school
   - early career decisions – how they were made

- key relationships
- things you made happen
- regrets
- major turning points in your life
- highlights and proudest moments
- your toughest challenges and how you dealt with them.

> **TIP** In your writing, express your thoughts and opinions on your story, as well as the facts.

## MY AUTOBIOGRAPHY

(Continued)

## ✳ Example

### Age 0–7

Earliest I can remember is sitting on the lawn at our old house looking at the sky. From an early age really loved football, would kick one around for hours. Always had a lot of energy and mum used to describe me as a tornado – always rushing around at full speed.

### Age 7–14

Remember doing quite well at primary school. I remember coming top of the class in the maths test and people being pleased with me. I think mum and dad were hoping I might get into the local grammar school but when I failed the test they were really supportive and told me that it didn't matter. I was a bit disappointed, but not overly because lots of my friends were going to the local comprehensive which made up for it. However, at secondary school more interested in football than anything else so I didn't pay much attention in class.

### Age 14–21

Got in with the anti-school crowd. Mum and dad got divorced when I was 15 but I was mainly just ignoring them anyway, making sure that I was out of the house and not in the middle of one of their arguments. I suddenly became the 'man of the house' – bit resentful but in some ways it did make me grow up. Became really important to bring money into the house so when I left school at 16 took the first job I could get that would pay money right away. Couldn't go into higher education even if I'd wanted to.

First few years at work was just working to get the money in – to bring money home and pay for my social life. Didn't think about having a career.

### Age 21–28

Found a new job at Peterson's and had a really good manager who I think spotted something in me. Really encouraged me – and I started to feel that maybe I did have career prospects. Got promoted and this did wonders for my confidence. However, aware of a bit of a glass ceiling for those who didn't start on the graduate programme with the company and knew I could only progress so far. Stayed two years

*(Continued)*

but then decided to join Smith's where I could get rewarded on results rather than qualifications. Especially important as getting married and the money to build a life together was important.

## Age 28–35

Had been doing really well in sales and getting increasingly interested in marketing. But same old problem of qualifications came up – I was never going to get the opportunity to get my manager's job without a sales and marketing qualification. Very reluctant to do it. What if I failed it? Where would that leave me? Actually decided to leave and work for smaller company where qualifications not so important. Regret this I think. If I'd have done the qualification earlier it would have been tough, but in the long run would probably have been worth it.

## Age 35–42

Have two kids and wife not working. Still considering whether or not I should study for a qualification. Hugely expensive and not sure whether I have the time to commit to it. Feel I haven't progressed as far as I should because of my lack of qualifications. Have steered clear of bigger companies because I don't think I stand a chance of being hired, even though I think I could do a much better job than the managers who are there already.

*Ralph*

You may have found Exercises 8 and 9 cathartic; a way of looking back on your career so far – the highs and the lows. Bear these in mind through the next chapter, and when you come to complete exercise 12 (p71), which is the reflections exercise for Part 2.

You will have been able to see from your autobiography the range of different influences as well as events that have shaped your history to date. We are going to examine those influences in more detail in the next chapter. These influences will have had great power in the past and many will continue to do so in the future. They are probably shaping your career right now, without you even being aware of it.

# 6 KEY CAREER INFLUENCES

I n your autobiography in Exercise 9, you saw how your personal life and your career are interwoven and that there are many influences that have shaped your decisions and life story.

These will have included the people, such as parents, teachers, friends, colleagues, partners and role models, who had a formative effect on your view of the world and your place within it.

External factors such as location, culture, class and educational routes may also have played their part in setting our expectations, steering our choices and presenting barriers or opportunities.

Some of these influences are so deep-rooted in our make-up that we have completely absorbed them and they are inseparable from who we are; whereas other influences we may be happy to discard as it suits us.

This chapter will get you thinking about the influences that have been and still continue to be very powerful for you with respect to your career. If you are aware of them, it at least gives you the opportunity to decide whether you want them to influence your next career decision or not.

Read through the influences below, and consider the questions. In Exercise 10 on p61 we'll be consolidating these answers.

## *Your family*

When you were growing up, your family will have helped shape your sense of identity and interpreted the external world for you. Our parents will have drawn our earliest boundaries, instilled the 'dos' and 'don'ts' and we would have started to define our sense of who we are and how the world operates by mirroring their own. Those early 'ground rules' are likely to be embedded somewhere in our consciousness.

The family is often very influential when it comes to making early career choices. This is understandable. At an early age, with little or no career experience, how can a student be expected to make fundamental career decisions based on

> My mum and dad were very modest really – not what you call high-flyers. But when I was the first one in my family to go to university, they were so proud. It made me feel exceptional. My upbringing I think has given me great personal self-confidence – that I can do well because of me and my efforts, not because of privilege. **Jim**

perhaps one meeting with a career adviser and some leaflets? Young people will look to adults they trust for guidance.

The expectations of the family can be very powerful. There may have been pressure for you to do well at school, to pursue a

> Both my parents were teachers, so it just seemed to be a natural choice. **Samantha**

particular kind of career path or even to follow in the family business. On the other hand, if they had a 'hands-free' or even uninterested approach, was this a hindrance, or did it in fact motivate you even more?

I often speak with individuals who had wanted to pursue a creative career but who were dissuaded by their parents who saw it as impractical. For some individuals this expresses itself as deep frustration and continuing regrets for a career they never pursued; while others are retrospectively grateful for the advice.

Think about what your parents expected of you.

# Community

If you have a strong community identity, whether this is faith-based, cultural, or geographical, the values of that community may also influence the kinds of job you seek and the organisations you want to work for. For instance you may need to take into account religious considerations in respect of the kind of organisations you want to work for.

What did your community expect of you?

> Brought up in a farming community, I have a natural love of the countryside and feel quite close to nature. I can't understand why people like being stuck in an office. **Jo**

> In my community, parents want their children to be a doctor or lawyer and will push them as hard as they can to achieve this. Anything else is a compromise. **Nita**

# Gender

The vast majority of jobs are equally open to men or women

However, even now some occupations are dominated by one gender or another, for example nursing and engineering. Is this because these jobs require abilities and traits that are more widely evident in either men or women, or because of society's influence?

And what happens if you choose to work in an area where the gender balance is swung in a different direction, if, for example you are a male nurse, female car mechanic or CEO of a FTSE 100 company?

Have you ever thought about whether the fact that you are male or female has affected your career choices and subsequent progress?

> I've always worked in very male-dominated environments where there was definitely sexism. However, if you are good, then as a woman you stand out much more, and you can definitely use that to your advantage. **Ruth Lea, Economist**

Women are not fulfilling their potential. Lots of women don't think about football; they don't think about construction as a career path. Really it's about opening people's minds to make them realise these are male jobs traditionally, but they don't need to be.

*Karren Brady, Vice-chairman, West Ham*

# Partner

Romantic relationships, current and past, may also have influenced your career to date. You may have made career choices that enabled you to be closer to your partner or even decided to set up business together. Your partner may have been incredibly supportive in respect of your career or could have been dismissive or over-reliant on you being the breadwinner. Raising children may also have required a re-balancing of your career priorities within the household.

How have your romantic relationships affected your career decisions?

I have to travel a lot for work and I know that my partner finds this really difficult as she has to do her job and look after the kids. However, if I want to get ahead, I'm going to need to do more travelling, not less. Which do I put first – family or career?     *Andy*

I know that if it wasn't for my husband I would never have dreamed of setting up my own business. He has been incredibly supportive and has helped me with the things I dreaded, for example VAT. Without him it wouldn't have been possible.     *Shirley*

# Educational experiences

Your experiences at school are likely to feature some of your earliest brushes with success and failure. How did your educational achievements compare with your expectations? Did you do better than you or your family thought? Or were you or they disappointed?

I coach many people who feel aggrieved and apologetic about their lack of academic success. Some of them have used it as a driver to prove their capabilities to the world and have become extremely successful. Others continue to struggle even into later life. For instance, it's very common for individuals who do have hang-ups about their qualifications to draw attention to their poor results in their job applications, rather than down-playing them. I've lost count of the times that I have seen CVs from mature people highlighting their unimpressive school exam results.

Your own perception of your academic success or lack of it is sometimes more of an influence on your subsequent career success than the actual qualifications themselves.

However, if you do want to something about it – and there are some jobs where a degree or vocational qualification is a definite advantage – the huge growth in part-time and distance-learning courses means that it is easier than ever to go back to academic learning if you want to.

So how do you feel about your academic achievements?

> I did exceptionally well at school. Always used to being the top of my class. I expected to get a first at university. But when I got a 2:1 instead I was very disappointed. I felt very ordinary and I had a real crisis of confidence. This definitely didn't help when I went for interviews.
>
> **Ben**

> I was so proud to get my degree. For me it showed the world that I could do it – that I had potential and I was as good as anyone else.
>
> **Margaret**

> I get so fed up of graduates who expect the world to fall at their feet. I didn't go to university but learned while on the job and have done really well. Common sense and hard work is what gets people on – not a paper qualification.
>
> **Martin**

# Role models

In our careers, we will have come across both good and bad role models: managers who were the embodiment of good leadership; and those who were pretty dreadful. We are likely to have picked up some good and bad habits from both.

There may be other role models who influenced you, perhaps a relative, someone in your community or even someone famous.

Who have your role models been?

> I have a colleague who has a great ability to calm down any fraught situation. She stays calm herself, uses humour, and really listens to the other person. Whenever I'm in a similar situation, I use some of the same tactics that I learned from observing her.  **Jane**

> My first boss was always ruthlessly honest. It made you work really hard to get his approval. I don't think I've ever worked so hard for anyone. I've always tried to use that same approach. People don't always like it, but I think they respect it  **Chris**

# Media

We are all influenced by popular culture, what we see on television or read about in the papers or on the internet. We see a range of different jobs and occupations represented in television dramas and documentaries. Whether the portrayal is accurate or not, these can often prove to be a powerful influence on our early career decisions.

For instance, the popularity of programmes like *Silent Witness* and *CSI* has led to a massive increase in the number of students wishing to train in forensic science, despite the relatively low number of job opportunities available.

Were any of your career choices or decisions based on what you had seen in the media – and were your preconceptions borne out in reality?

Where did your ambitions stem from?

> I always wanted to work in fashion. I lapped up the glossy magazines, was glued to programmes about fashion like a magpie. My salary has always gone on clothes. I know it's superficial, but my priority is working for a 'cool brand' over practically anything else
> **Gemma**

> Saw a documentary about an animal sanctuary when I was a young boy and I knew then that I wanted to work with animals. They have always been a major part of both my working life and home life.
> **Andrew**

# Wider society

We are all affected by changes in the political and economic landscape. In tough times, intense competition for jobs may require compromises in our career choices. The graduate schemes that were available last year may no longer be there. The promotional opportunities we hoped for may have disappeared as the organisation sheds staff in order to stay afloat during an economic downturn.

Recent changes in our society have affected the job market and therefore our career possibilities, for example:

- the abolition of the compulsory retirement age means important new rights for older workers
- the increase in university tuition fees is likely to mean fewer undergraduates and therefore greater competition for entry-level jobs.
- the public sector cuts mean limited recruitment in many areas including councils, the NHS, education, the police force and charities.

So if you think about your career in the past, there will be many ways in which the political and economic landscape has affected your working life. How have you fared with the economic ups and downs within your industry?

# Exercise 10: Your career influences

**10**

| Practical influences | People influences | Wider influences |
|---|---|---|
| Financial | Parents | Cultural |
| Security | Family | Community |
| Location | Peers/colleagues | Religious |
| Job availability | Friends | Political |
| Qualifications | Teachers | Media |
| Career experiences | Role models | Gender |
| Disability | Partner | Social class |
| Training | Managers | Discrimination |

1. From the lists above, write down below which factors you believe have had an influence on your career to date and why.
2. How do you think those influences affected you in comparison with those in a similar position, such as your siblings or peers?
3. Which of these influences do you believe will continue to be influential for you in the future?
4. There is an example of this exercise on pp62–3.

## MY INFLUENCES

*(Continued)*

[ ]

## ✴ Example

### MY INFLUENCES

**Family** – they discouraged me from pursuing art, which I really wanted to do, as they didn't see it as a proper job.

**Gender** – as a man I think there is an expectation that I will always be the breadwinner and that this is my responsibility above everything else.

**Social class** – my father didn't think that an 'artistic' job was a proper job for a man.

**Art teacher** – was wonderful. Very supportive. Only increased my frustration with my parents.

**Location** – took first job which would take me away from home so that I could live my own life.

**Career experiences** – found that marketing at least had some creativity to it.

*(Continued)*

**Partner** – she relies on me to be the breadwinner but sometimes I think why can't she go out to work and I will stay at home, look after the kids and paint.

**Role model** – my kids. I love the way they play with paint, they are so free and spontaneous.

**Peers** – I'm not that interested in my peers at work. Benchmark myself against fellow artists.

My brother and sister have all followed very conventional careers and been very successful. Have always really struggled to throw off that sense of frustration – that I haven't been able to follow my heart and do a job that I've loved. Work has always been solely about bringing the money in – nothing else; and this is largely how I continue to think about work.

I wonder, though, whether there is some other role that I can do, which would interest me more than my current job but which was realistic salary-wise?

*Ray*

This chapter has shown that your choices in your career are likely to have been heavily influenced by a range of personal and societal factors. Some of these will still be very relevant, while others may have been discarded or replaced over time.

Are you surprised by your answers to Exercise 10? Perhaps you didn't realise your family had such a strong influence on your past career choice, or noticed that your desire to change jobs has come from a specific role model who inspires you. Whatever's struck you, keep this in mind as you work through the rest of Part 2.

# 7  YOUR CAREER HISTORY

E mployers pay very close attention to your job history because they want to understand not only whether you have the skills and experience to fill their vacancy, but also the rationale for your career decisions, your personal development and your relationships with previous employers.

In this chapter we are going to put a magnifying glass up to each job you've worked in and examine it closely. You need to understand your job history if you are to explain it to anyone else. Analysing your job experiences will also reveal any common themes about your likes, dislikes and any recurrent challenges.

Don't worry if your career to date has not followed what you think is a standard pattern. Many people change their career focus, not just while they are experimenting in the early stages of their career, but increasingly mid-career too.

In addition, most people will have had career breaks, career mistakes, periods of unemployment, temporary or voluntary jobs along the way. These are the standard features of most modern careers rather than the exception.

Whatever your career experiences have been, all of them will have provided intense learning experiences, testing your capabilities, extending your knowledge and exposing you to other career possibilities.

So let's look chronologically at your different work experiences and what they tell us about you.

# Exercise 11: Your work history ⬇

1. Consider every paid role you have undertaken. For each role, write down the following in the space below.
   - How did you get this job?
   - What did you like and dislike about it?
   - What did you learn?
   - Why did you leave?

> **TIP** Think about what you knew at the end of your job that you didn't know at the beginning.

2. If you have limited paid work experience, you can also include any unpaid work experience, placements, voluntary work or similar.

3. If you need more space to write, complete this exercise on a separate piece of paper or on your computer.

4. There is an example on p66.

> **TIP** To make this exercise easier, use a current CV to help remind you of your past jobs.

Role No. 1

Role No. 2

*(Continued)*

Role No. 3

Role No. 4

Role No. 5

## ✷ *Example*

### Role no. 1

Trainee at Smith's Management Consultants
Heard about the job through my friend John. Liked fact that I had a
relatively easy entry into organisation – made me feel a bit special.
For couple of years I was really very happy – doing well, they seemed to
think highly of me. Introduced new management systems so company
had accurate information rather than using guesswork. Organised
the company relocation – massive task but went well. Grew my team.
Learned about people management. Only left because I outgrew the role.

*Joshua*

**TIP** We will revisit this exercise when we create your Career Summary
document on p245.

Looking at your entire career history to date, let's start to debrief this exercise to ascertain what we can learn from looking at your job history as a whole.

## ✕ *Examining your roles*

Reviewing your work history, write your answers to the following questions in the box below.

1. How have you have typically found a new job? For example, through a personal contact or agency? This will be useful for thinking about how you might find your next job.
2. What were the differences between the jobs you enjoyed and those you didn't? Look for common themes in the jobs you enjoyed. What differentiated them from the other jobs?
3. Were there any difficulties which surfaced in more than one job, for example bullying or a difficult workplace relationship?

1. How have you typically found a new job?

2. What were the differences between the jobs you enjoyed and those you didn't?

3. Were there any difficulties which surfaced in more than one job, for example bullying or a difficult workplace relationship?

## ✳ Example

---

1. **How have you typically found a new job?**

I found most of my roles through hearing about them from someone I know.

2. **What were the differences between the jobs you enjoyed and those you didn't?**

Career highlights were working in the TV production company. Loved it. Exciting. Fast-moving. Got to meet lots of interesting people. Very lively. Also working on the conferences for Jays. Liked being front of house – doing the PR.

Got very miserable in a couple of jobs and stayed there far longer than I should. Only moved in the end because the threat of redundancy eventually spurred me on. Not very proactive.

The jobs I enjoyed all involved working with people who were great fun. They made me laugh. Lots of energy. Used to socialise after work. Great team spirit. Worked hard. Played hard.

Jobs where I was unhappy were ones where I felt that my personality just didn't suit the company. Felt like a fish out of water. Didn't have my sense of humour. Just didn't seem to connect. They were far too straight for me.

3. **Were there any difficulties which surfaced in more than one job, for example bullying or a difficult workplace relationship?**

Some organisations just didn't feel like I fitted in – they were much too corporate for me. I like a more relaxed atmosphere.

*Joshua*

---

# Career luck or career design?

I hope that what you have started to see emerging in this section is a sense of how your career and the person you are today has been shaped by how you have responded to a wide range of influences, events and circumstances.

Even if you feel that your career to date has happened more by accident than design, you will have chosen to accept certain opportunities and not others when you saw them. You will have decided to tackle certain career problems while you may have run away from others. You may have put yourself in the way of potential opportunities or hidden yourself from view. Even a decision to do nothing at all is a decision.

You are not where you are solely by chance!

Professor Richard Wiseman's book *The Luck Factor* (Arrow, 2004) was written following his innovative research into why some individuals seem to have better luck than

> In my last job everyone was constantly whinging and moaning about the organisation. It was relentless and very depressing. I didn't want to work in such a negative environment so I worked hard to get myself out as quickly as I could. Why are the others still there if they are so unhappy?
>
> **Pam**

others. He examined the actual beliefs and experiences of lucky and unlucky people. From his research he distilled four simple techniques commonly used by lucky people. You may not win the lottery with his techniques, but his research showed that these behaviours can undoubtedly influence the odds as to whether good things are likely to happen to you.

## MAXIMISE CHANCE OPPORTUNITIES

Lucky people are skilled at creating, noticing and acting upon chance opportunities. They do this in various ways, including networking, adopting a relaxed attitude to life and by being open to new experiences.

## LISTEN TO LUCKY HUNCHES

Lucky people make effective decisions by listening to their intuition and gut feelings. In addition, they take steps to actively boost their intuitive abilities by, for example, meditating and clearing their mind of other thoughts.

## EXPECT GOOD FORTUNE

Lucky people are certain that the future is going to be full of good fortune. These expectations become self-fulfilling prophecies by helping lucky people persist in the face of failure and shape their interactions with others in a positive way.

*(Continued)*

## TURN BAD LUCK TO GOOD

Lucky people employ various psychological techniques to cope with, and often even thrive upon, the ill fortune that comes their way. For example, they spontaneously imagine how things could have been worse, do not dwell on their ill fortune, and take control of the situation.

*Professor Richard Wiseman, The Luck Factor (Arrow, 2004)*

> Luck is what happens when preparation meets opportunity. **Seneca**

Now think about all the times in your career when you felt that you had a lucky break. You may have had a chance meeting with someone who later hired you or your application landed on the manager's desk just when they were looking for someone like you.

> Luck has a peculiar habit of favouring those who don't depend on it. **Anon**

Was it just luck? The opportunity may have landed at your feet, but you needed to capitalise on it. You would still have had to impress the employer that you could do the job. You would have needed to take the initiative to make the application or decide to talk to the stranger in the room. The risky job move that worked out brilliantly you could have rejected because you wanted to play safe. If you hadn't decided to push for management training with your employer, then perhaps you would never have been ready to step into your boss's shoes when they left unexpectedly.

In your career, you make your own luck!

## *Looking at your history*

This chapter has been a fairly intense and detailed look at your personal and career history. We have looked at the key events, your life story, major influences and your career experiences.

# *Exercise 12: Reflecting on Part 2*

Review the following exercises:

- Exercise 8: My life events (p44)
- Exercise 9: Your autobiography (p49)
- Exercise 10: Your career influences (p61)
- Exercise 11: Your work history (p65)

Note down any other thoughts or observations that are prompted when you read your own words. These might include:

1. What you have learned about yourself from these exercises.
2. What positive things about you have emerged from these exercises.
3. What advice you might have given to your past self.
4. Are there things you would do differently in the future?
5. What actions can you take that will make a difference?

There is space for you to write down your thoughts on p72.

### ✵ My reflections on my history

### ✵ Action points

## ✳ Example: my reflections on my history

I'm thankful to my parents for pushing me hard. Even now I hate to do anything that might disappoint my parents. Friends are definitely a big influence. I am competitive so I do want to do better than them career-wise. I don't want to get left behind. Salary is a benchmark for me in this. If I can keep up with or exceed the salary of my friends then I feel I am doing well. I can see that I am quite an impatient person. On the one hand, this is good because it has meant that if something isn't right then I've quickly done something about it. But on occasion I think that I jumped too fast. I knew that I didn't want what I had, so I looked for the fastest way out, rather than thinking about what was the right next move for me. I have been like this in my jobs but also my relationships too. Maybe I need to slow down a bit. Think before I jump.

## ✳ Example: action points

1. Slow down my decision-making
2. Do my research more thoroughly on any new job before I accept it
3. Research typical salary levels for those in my field to draw comparison

*Alex*

**TIP** We will revisit this reflections exercise when we look back on your career coaching journey in Exercise 48, p250.

# What you can offer: your career capital

## PART 3

L et me introduce you to a concept called 'career capital'. Put simply, career capital is the skills, knowledge and attributes that you have to offer a potential employer. This is also often called your 'employability'. The value of your career capital will depend on its relevance to a particular job, employer demand and expectations, and how you compare with other candidates in the job market.

## In this section we will:

✓ identify what skills you already possess

✓ understand what value you bring to a company

✓ look at your experience, training and professional credibility

✓ discover other elements that enhance your career capital.

# 8 IDENTIFYING YOUR SKILLS

Whatever path your career coaching leads you on – be it a new job, promotion, or change of career entirely, the skills you possess will help you get to where you want to be.

These will include specific work-related skills which you know you do well, others you have learnt to acquire, as well as some which you simply take for granted.

## Competencies

You may hear employers refer to skills as 'competencies'. Employers often prefer this term because instead of describing a generic skill, a competence is very practical, showing how that skill has been applied in real-life scenarios. The different terminology reflects the difference between a medical receptionist saying, for instance, they are 'good with people' (skill) or 'experienced in dealing with visitors to the surgery who can be very anxious' (competency-based statement).

Whenever employers are looking to recruit new staff they will specify the particular skills they are looking for. They will usually describe these in job advertisements and the person specification forms that are often attached to job descriptions. When they are considering your CV and questioning you at interview, they will be looking for practical examples of how you have demonstrated the skills they are looking for in your past roles.

## *Transferable skills*

If you are considering a change in role or sector, then taking a closer look at the skills you possess can help you pinpoint your transferable skills. These transferable skills will be invaluable to you if you want to change sector or are making a large career overhaul.

> I worked for 20 years for the council in planning permission and panicked that I would never find another job when I was made redundant. However, when we started to look at my transferable skills, I could see that I am very experienced at dealing with all the complex paperwork and procedures around property issues and good at explaining it to home-owners. I've now working at my local estate agent, which I am really enjoying, where my skills are very relevant.                    **Claire**

Transferable skills are those which you have been using in one environment but which you can apply to another. An example might be project management, where you can use your organisational, people and planning skills in other contexts.

## *Exercise 13: Skills assessment*

This exercise will help you identify your strongest skills.

Very few people are good at everything, so be very selective in the skills you choose. Identify the skills you excel at, rather than those you just loosely possess.

This exercise will also help you decide which skills you are interested in using for the future. Sometimes you may be very good at something; you just don't want to do it any more.

1.  Using a coloured pen, highlight which, in your opinion, are your 5–10 top skills. The skills list isn't exhaustive, but it is designed as a useful prompt. Feel free to add any other skills you have that are not on the list.

| | | |
|---|---|---|
| Adapting | Co-ordinating | Enforcing |
| Administering | Coping | Estimating |
| Advising | Counselling | Evaluating |
| Analysing | Creating | Examining |
| Anticipating | Cultivating | Experimenting |
| Appraising | Customer service | Explaining |
| Articulating | Decision-making | Facilitating |
| Assembling | Delegating | Filing |
| Assessing | Demonstrating | Finalising |
| Auditing | Designing | Financing |
| Briefing | Detailing | Fixing |
| Budgeting | Detecting | Forecasting |
| Building | Developing | Generating ideas |
| Calculating | Diagnosing | Growing plants |
| Certifying | Diplomacy | Guiding |
| Chairing | Directing | Handling conflict |
| Classifying | Displaying | Helping |
| Coaching | Disproving | Illustrating |
| Collaborating | Dissecting | Implementing |
| Collating | Disseminating | Improving |
| Communicating (face to face) | Documenting | Improvising |
| | Drafting | Influencing |
| Communicating (telephone) | Drawing | Informing |
| | Driving | Initiating |
| Computing | Editing | Innovating |
| Conceptualising | Educating | Inspecting |
| Constructing | Empathising | Inspiring |
| Consulting | Empowering | Installing |
| Controlling | | |

*(Continued)*

| | | |
|---|---|---|
| Interpreting | Ordering | Representing |
| Interviewing | Organising | Researching |
| Inventing | Painting | Restoring |
| Investigating | Persuading | Risk assessment |
| Judging | Piloting | Scheduling |
| Launching | Pioneering | Selling |
| Leading | Planning | Setting objectives |
| Learning quickly | Precision | Simplifying |
| Lecturing | Presenting | Sorting |
| Liaising | Prioritising | Structuring |
| Lifting | Problem-solving | Summarising |
| Listening | Procuring | Supervising |
| Making presentations | Promoting | Systematising |
| Managing | Proofreading | Teaching |
| Managing people | Public speaking | Team building |
| Marketing | Publicising | Testing |
| Measuring | Purchasing | Time management |
| Mediating | Quantifying | Training |
| Memorising | Raising animals | Trouble-shooting |
| Mentoring | Reconciling | Using tools |
| Modelling | Recording | Versatility |
| Moderating | Recruiting | Visualising |
| Motivating | Rehabilitating | Winning |
| Negotiating | Relationship building | Working to deadlines |
| Networking | Repairing | Working under pressure |
| Operating | Report writing | Writing |

**2.** Now use a different coloured pen to circle which of these skills you particularly want to use in the future. For the skills you have identified as your best skills, think of examples when you have demonstrated your skills in action. These may be skills you use every day or occasionally.

| Your key skills | Examples of when you have used these skills |
|---|---|
| 1 | |
| 2 | |
| 3 | |
| 4 | |
| 5 | |

**3.** Now identify any skills that you want to develop further. Perhaps these will help you to do your current job better, improve your promotion prospects or are skills that simply interest you.

---

Skills I want to develop further

---

## ✯ Example

| Your key skills | Examples of when you have used these skills |
|---|---|
| 1 Communicating in writing | Wrote all the communications to customers informing them of the takeover<br>Wrote copy for the website<br>Produced reports for management |

---

Skills I want to develop further

My presentation skills. Dealing with difficult people. Handling journalists.

---

Your skills are one of the most important aspects of your career capital and this exercise will prove very useful when you need to persuade employers of your suitability, or when you are assessing your options. The skills you have noted will help you decide whether you are capable of what you want to achieve right now or if there are gaps you need to close.

Later in Part 3 we will also be asking others for their input on what they think your skills are, as it is highly likely there will be others that you have missed.

# 9 ADDING VALUE

To get more of an idea of what you can offer employers, we're going to look at your past performance. Where have you proved your worth, or added value to the companies you have been working for?

Let's take a look at this from the employer's perspective. Employees are expensive. They are costly and time-consuming to hire and in addition to their salary there are a whole host of other associated costs including induction, training, annual leave and sickness cover.

Every employer dreads taking on a 'problem' employee because this can be costly, energy-draining and potentially damaging to the organisation. Most people have had experience of a 'problem' member of staff, and if you have, you can appreciate just how difficult it can be.

Employers tend to view most candidates cautiously to see if there are any tell-tale signs that give clues as to whether they are in the 'problem' camp or in the 'star player' camp. So if you think that employers are giving you a hard time at interview, they are, and it's their job – to protect the organisation and ensure that they invest the organisation's money in the right person.

This means that the more you can show an employer that you are a safe pair of hands and that you have added value to organisations where you have worked in the past, the more attractive you become. This is essential if you are thinking of moving jobs.

Employers are particularly interested in examples of when you have been able to:

- increase profits
- reduce costs
- sell more
- solve a problem
- improve efficiency
- raise quality
- generate ideas
- enhance customer satisfaction.

This chapter will help you gather the evidence that you can 'add value' to a company, by looking at your achievements and the positive impact you have made in the past.

This will help present you as a person who:

- does over and above what is required in the role
- can see how your effort relates to the bigger organisational picture
- is results-focused
- likes a challenge
- gets things done.

This chapter is equally relevant if you are thinking about another career move, whether working for yourself or progressing in your current role. The outcome of this chapter will give you hard evidence of the things you have achieved in your work life – and hopefully a confidence boost too.

## So what have you achieved?

No matter what roles you have been working in or how long your career has been, there will be a number of achievements that you have been responsible for and ways that you have added value to the organisation you worked for. It's very common for individuals to be overly modest about their contribution. For instance, I have worked with many coaching clients over the years who have won awards for their work, but who never thought to mention them either on their CV or at interview. In the following exercise, you have permission to put all modesty aside and 'blow your own trumpet'.

Complete the following exercise to help you start you thinking about some of your biggest achievements.

# Exercise 14: Identifying your ⬇ achievements

## 14

1. Use the box below to spontaneously list several achievements in your career which you found particularly satisfying or that other people seemed to rate highly. Ideally make them work-related, although you can include a couple of personal achievements too. Your achievements could include things such as the following.
   - Awards, commendations, special mentions, for example being top sales person.
   - Solving a problem that needed addressing, such as improving customer relations.
   - Taking a calculated risk which paid off, for example negotiating a new deal.
   - Being given responsibility for a difficult task, such as closing a factory.
   - Making improvements, for example redesigning a website.
   - Your proudest moments at work, such as launching a new product
   - Personal challenges such as project-managing the building of your house.

> **TIP** It doesn't have to be an achievement where you were solely responsible for the outcome. Choose examples where your contribution was significant, either to you or to the organisation.

You might also find it helpful to dig out past appraisals or any other documents or emails that provide positive feedback on your achievements.

MY ACHIEVEMENTS

*(Continued)*

2. From your list above, select a minimum of three achievements and start to explore each of these in more detail, noting down your answers to the following questions.
   - Why are you particularly proud of this achievement?
   - What was difficult about it?
   - What did you do that made a difference?
   - Why did it matter to you, the organisation, to others?

3. There is an example on p88.

Achievement 1:

(Continued)

Achievement 2:

Achievement 3:

Achievement 4:

### ✴ Example

I was asked to be the acting manager when my boss went on sick leave. We didn't know how long she was going to be away. I was very new in post but felt very nervous. However, I got stuck in. It was a bit of a baptism by fire because there were lots of things I just didn't know but I was honest and I became very resourceful at finding out the answers. The other staff were very helpful and supportive – it would have been a nightmare if they hadn't been – but I think they could see I was doing my best and wanted to help me. I did this role for six months and it was fantastic personal development. I know that I also held the department together at what could have been a very tricky time. They gave me an extra payment to reflect my input. I felt pleased that I was able to do a decent job when I was, to be frank, completely out of my depth, and it gave me real confidence that I would be able to manage at that more senior level. The organisation benefited in that they clearly saved money by not having to recruit someone temporarily into the role. They could also see that I was an additional resource they could use over and above the role I was appointed to – and so I was assigned to sit on the Working Group project team.

*Lara*

**4.** Once you have explored the detail of your key achievements, consider the following and write your thoughts below.

Are there any common elements in the different achievements you have chosen?

*(Continued)*

What do they say about you to a potential employer?

## ✳ Example

Are there any common elements in the different achievements you have chosen?

All of my achievements show an ability to bring order and structure to an uncertain situation. I'm good at dealing with ambiguity and seeing where we need to go and providing a path to lead us there. I like getting things organised. Working on projects is great.

What do they say about you to a potential employer?

I have excellent organisational skills. You can give me a mess and I will sort it out. Give me your problems and I will enjoy the challenge.

*Mark*

# Demonstrating your worth

Your achievements are just a few examples of the positive contribution you have made to the organisations you have worked with.

There are likely to be many others where you have demonstrated your worth to your employers. They may be less personally satisfying than those in your achievements exercise above, and may be part of your everyday responsibilities, but they are equally of interest. Here are some examples.

- Updating a website which increased customer hits by 10%.
- Changing the method of data input to increase database accuracy.
- Revamping a shop window so that it attracted more customers.
- Reducing staff turnover by 5% by introducing a new absence policy.
- Developing new services that generated £20,000 of business in the first month.
- Managing a complex new building project with zero accidents.
- Reorganising a database system to reflect changing management needs.
- Developing a high-performance team including existing under-performing staff.

> You don't get paid for the hour. You get paid for the value you bring to the hour.
> *Jim Rohn*

No matter what job you have worked in, there will always be things you have done that have left the job/team/organisation in a better place than when you arrived. This is very important information for your career capital, regardless of whether you worked for a commercial organisation, a charity or the public sector.

> As an administrator I struggled to see how I had 'added value' to the organisation. However, when I started to think about it, there were lots of things that I had done which were important. If I didn't get the invoices out on time, the company's cash flow could have been jeopardised. If I didn't take customer contact details accurately, a potential sale could have been lost. *Harmeet*

However, when you are so close to your role and perhaps unused to working in a commercial environment, it can sometimes be tricky to see the wider impact that you have. In this case, you might find it helpful to imagine a scenario where no one was doing your role, or they were doing it extremely badly. What might go wrong? What would the risks to the organisation be? What would the negative consequences be? By doing this you will see that you have been doing a whole host of things that have had a positive impact.

Where you can, try to research whether your department or organisation has any facts and figures that can substantiate the value of the improvements you made. Look at your departmental targets, management reports, sales figures and your performance evaluations for relevant information.

> **TIP** From now on, make a note of new examples of your positive impact at work, so that you have a list that is continuously updated.

# Exercise 15: Adding value ⬇

**15**

1. Think of a minimum of four examples in both your current and last job where you helped to add value to the organisation.

2. Include any numbers, figures or percentages that you can to illustrate the impact. It can be approximate if you don't know the exact amount.

3. If relevant, you can also include voluntary work, placements or extra-curricular activities where you have demonstrated your worth.

> **TIP** Don't just rush through this exercise – take time to gather facts and information so that you have a complete picture of where you have added value, and some evidence to support it.

| Company | How you added value |
| --- | --- |
| | |
| | |
| | |
| | |

## ✻ Example

| Company | How you added value |
|---------|---------------------|
| Jones | Developed new email policy which reduced the amount of time staff were spending on non-work related websites. Introduced e-learning which minimised time staff spent out of the office, replacing one-day course with six 30-minute sessions. Negotiated new deal with stationery suppliers which achieved £500 per month in savings. |
| Smith | Introduced new customer worth £20k to the company. Reorganised workload of team which reduced staff headcount with savings of £25k. *Stephanie* |

In this chapter we have looked at how you can show an employer that you are an asset to your organisation, rather than a cost, and that in the role you are a high performer rather than a 'jobsworth'.

What you've collected together is valuable information that can be used to remind your current employer of your contribution, perhaps to justify a promotion or a pay rise. It will also be very relevant when you want to impress potential new employers.

# 10 WORKING OUT WHAT YOU KNOW

Your know-how or expertise are a key part of your career offering. Some of it may be transferable to a range of different scenarios, while some will be very context-specific. For example, being an expert on tomato horticulture doesn't necessarily make you a landscape gardener; whereas IT skills like Excel can be used in many organisations.

Interestingly, many coaching clients I work with, especially those who are in a non-specialist role, take their knowledge for granted. It's almost as though it is so embedded in their head that they lose sight of it.

For your career capital to retain its value, your knowledge has to be continuously updated. This might mean going on top-up courses, reading journals, attending conferences or professional events. You could be the most highly qualified person in your organisation, but if you've not kept abreast of developments in your field, you could be a liability. For example who would want to employ an HR officer who doesn't know about the latest employment legislation or an administrator who can only use an old software package?

> I didn't realise at first that I was an expert in anything, but then it came up that one of my main duties is arranging exports and I guess I am very knowledgeable about this, having done it for 20 years. *Christine*

In this chapter, we are going to capture on paper what you know. This will include looking at your key areas of knowledge and your learning and development activities' as well as your qualifications and any professional memberships.

## *Work-related qualifications*

An employer will place high value on any qualifications you have achieved that are directly relevant to the job you are applying for. The fact that you had to pass an exam, provide coursework or a portfolio to achieve the qualification is evidence that you have been independently judged to have achieved a certain level of appropriate knowledge.

**16**

## *Exercise 16: Your professional credibility*

### ✳ *Qualifications*

Write down all of your professional or vocational qualifications. These may include certificates, diplomas, NVQs, vocational degrees or postgraduate training.

### ✳ *Example*

Professional diploma in marketing
Certificate in professional sales practice
Level 7 qualification in executive management
Degree in business studies

*Chris*

## ✳ Professional memberships

List any memberships of professional organisations to which you belong, for example the General Medical Council or the Chartered Institute of Public Relations. Such organisations usually require members to work to certain standards and ethics. Also include any other work-related memberships which show that you take your professional commitments seriously, are keeping abreast of developments in the field and have contacts in your industry. Examples might include sitting on industry committees, cross-organisational working groups, research forums, quality groups or business forums.

## ✳ Example

Associate of the Chartered Institute of Personnel and Development (CIPD)
Member of the British Psychological Society
Member of the HR Charity Sector Forum
Member of local CIPD branch committee
Active member of CIPD local policy group

*Jenny*

# Training and development

Employers want to see that you have completed relevant training in the past and that your skills are up to date. If you can demonstrate that you are committed to continuous development, your career capital is likely to have greater value because it is more current.

Write down below all the training and development activities you have undertaken. Your training and development could include any of the following.

- In-house courses such as customer service, health and safety.
- External courses such as PRINCE2.
- E-learning packages such as MCSE Microsoft engineer packages.
- Extensive reading on particular subjects, for example corporate social responsibility.
- Being involved in the fast-track talent pool at work.
- Workplace coaching or mentoring.
- Distance learning.
- Attendance at conferences or seminars.
- Participation in action learning groups.
- Secondment opportunities.

## 17 *Exercise 17: Your training and development*

1. Write down all your training and development activities here.

2. Highlight any areas that need updating.

## ✳ Example

Two-day course in handling workplace conflict
Assertiveness course
On-the-job training on customer service desk
Presentation skills
Leadership training course
Investors in People training course
Handling disciplinary and grievance procedures
Equal opportunities
Need to update my understanding of recent legislation

*Alison*

# Your knowledge

As well as your qualifications and training, you will have gathered an amount of knowledge throughout your working life. This is just as valuable as the qualifications you have, but you need to be able to give specific examples to showcase your knowledge.

Think about your current and previous jobs. Imagine yourself in the role. What were the kind of things that people would ask your advice on? When would your input be required? What prior knowledge would a new recruit to your role be required to have? And what additional knowledge did you gain as a result of working there?

# *Exercise 18: Extracting your knowledge*

Try to identify for each job the knowledge you had that was important to the organisation. Examples could include:

- your technical expertise, for example management accounts
- knowledge about a particular product or service, for example mobile phones
- understanding of a particular industry or sector, for example local councils
- local or international knowledge, for example doing business in China
- cultural knowledge, for example working with different ethnic groups
- knowledge of systems and procedures, for example ISO quality standards
- research knowledge, for example clinical trials
- knowledge of particular customers, suppliers, for example SMEs.

Write down your key areas of knowledge below.

> **TIP** To help you do this exercise, refer back to Exercise 11 for your list of previous jobs.

## ✷ Example

International conference management

Sales and marketing

Webinars

Formulating business proposals

Chairing meetings

Service level agreements

Public sector procurement

Budget management

Recruitment

Managing a team

Performance incentives

*Chris*

In this chapter you will have documented the key elements of your career capital, from qualifications to learned knowledge. This will be useful in proving your professional credibility to a potential employer, and provide the basis of proving your worth – to yourself as well as an employer.

# 11 CAREER CAPITAL EXTRAS

There may be many other things, apart from your qualifications and training experiences, that you should count as part of your career capital. Examples could include any valuable experiences gained outside work, your privileged access to useful information or contacts, or the reputation you have built in your industry.

This chapter is designed to prompt you to think of anything else that you can offer that an employer would potentially value.

## *Non-work experiences*

> I have been involved in mentoring young people from socially disadvantaged backgrounds. It's been an eye-opener for me and immensely rewarding. It's also made me realise that my own horizons have been pretty narrow and that we need to be more inclusive both within our own organisation as well as in the services we provide. **Daniel**

Any experience where you were working in a relevant environment, taking the opportunity to develop your skills and abilities, or demonstrating your willingness to work hard and contribute, can be of potential interest to an employer.

For example, voluntary work is a great way to prove your work ethic, and it suggests that you have the kind of energy and community spirit that employers hope their staff will bring into the organisation with them. Some examples could include:

- organising a charity event
- internships or work placements
- helping in a friend's business
- sitting on a residents' committee
- mentoring vulnerable people
- organising the local football team.

## Exercise 19: Other work experience

**19**

 **Example**

> Been helping get sponsorship for the school fête – talking to local businesses, including the garden centre, who gave us lots of plants to sell. Helped organise local campaign to fight proposed building on green belt land.
>
> *Alison*

## Hobbies and interests

What hobbies or outside (non-work) interests do you have? Could these be of any relevance in respect of your future career? This doesn't necessarily

> I love classical music and so the chance to work as part of the marketing team for the opera company was just my dream job.
>
> *Liz*

mean pursuing your hobby professionally, but it could give you a way into an organisation that is connected with your hobby.

I've coached many clients whose career satisfaction has been transformed because they moved to a job in this way, including an accountant working for a golf club and a sales executive who moved into the film industry.

## Exercise 20: Your hobbies and interests

⋆ **Example**

> I'm interested in photography, computer games, cars, gadgets, iPhone apps.
>
> *Graham*

## Your networks

Your ability to access people, information and resources can form a key part of your career capital. If you know the key people in your industry, have relationships in place with potential customers, or those with influence in the sector, these can be used for the employer's benefit. For instance, people working in PR will be expected to have a range of suitable contacts. A sales person who already knows people who are likely to buy their product is at an advantage. Think about people you know or can get access to, including:

- potential customers – individuals, groups or organisations
- key industry players, such as large organisations in your field
- relevant decision-makers, for example local councils
- political representatives, such as MPs
- those who can give you information and access to resources
- trade bodies
- prestige contacts, for example VIPs, celebrities.

Write down here the people you know and the type of contacts you have that will be of great help in enabling you to do a good job for an organisation.

## Exercise 21: Your networks

### ✷ Example

Procurement manager at ZYS
Journalist with local paper
Rachel who sits on the board of trustees
Ben at the FSB
Jane who does the training
Ryan at the software company

*Rosie*

**22**

# Exercise 22: Additional information

Is there anything else you believe you can offer that would be of interest to a potential employer? For example:

- publications, blogs, articles that you write
- conference presentations you have given
- languages you speak.

✴ **Example**

I write a weekly blog on green issues and have stood as local councillor.

*Gary*

# Understanding your career capital

In Part 3 we have looked in detail at the many elements which comprise your career capital.

It is highly probable that your existing manager is unaware of many of the things you can offer. If there are areas of skill and knowledge that you are not currently using, but which could be of benefit to the organisation, this could be a great opportunity to get involved in some other interesting work activities. I remember working with a client who spoke several languages. It wasn't strictly relevant to the job she was doing, but she could see that it could be of real help when the company were arranging their international conference. They agreed and she proved to be so successful working alongside the event management team that a year later she moved to be a full member of that department.

Almost every client I have ever worked with has failed to appreciate the depth and breadth of their career capital. If you don't know the value of what you've got, you are in danger of underselling yourself.

---

**TIP** On p246 there is a section for you to fill in the key elements of your career capital in your Career Summary document. Turn to this page now and include the information you have collected from Part 3 so that you have an easily accessible record that you can turn to in the future.

---

# Exercise 23: Reflecting on Part 3

**23**

In this section you have gathered together a lot of information, covering many different areas, about your career capital.

Review the following exercises:

- Exercise 13: Skills assessment (p78)
- Exercise 14: Identifying your achievements (p85)
- Exercise 15: Adding value (p91)
- Exercise 16: Your professional credibility (p94)
- Exercise 17: Your training and development (p96)
- Exercise 18: Extracting your knowledge (p98)
- Exercise 19: Other work experience (p101)
- Exercise 20: Your hobbies and interests (p102)
- Exercise 21: Your networks (p103)
- Exercise 22: Additional information (p104)

Now complete the following reflections exercise. The idea of this exercise is to capture any thoughts you may have about the following.

- What have you learned about yourself from this section?
- What have you found difficult?
- Have you had any other thoughts or ideas during these exercises?
- Actions for you to take.

## ✳ *My reflections on what I can offer*

## ✳ *Action points*

## ⚝ Example: my reflections on what I can offer

When I looked at my career capital I must admit I felt quite impressed. There was more there than I thought there was.

I'd forgotten that I have a lot of knowledge about working with vulnerable people through my work with social services. It is very relevant for helping me deal with difficult customers in my current job because a lot of it was about handling conflict in a very helpful way.

## ⚝ Example: action points

1. Remind myself of all the things I have to offer as a confidence boost
2. Use the information gained from this section when writing my CV and for interview
3. Investigate courses to develop my skills further

*Sharon*

**TIP** We will revisit this reflections exercise when we look back on your career coaching journey in Exercise 48.

# All about you

So far we've looked at your current career situation, your personal and work history, and your career capital.

In Part 4, we are going to be finding out more about your personality and behaviours in the workplace. We are also going to gather feedback from your friends and colleagues to see how other people view you.

Whether you like it or not, a prospective employer makes a judgement about the kind of person they think you are, and whether you are a good fit for their organisation. If you are aware of your own workstyle you can actively seek organisations which work in a complementary way to your own approach.

## In this section we will:

✓ look at your personality type and how this affects your career

✓ discover what workstyle suits you

✓ get some feedback on how others see you.

# 12 **YOUR WORKSTYLE**

There are certain personal traits and behaviours that every employer will want their staff to have, regardless of the role. These include:

- reliability
- honesty
- flexibility
- energy
- being hardworking
- being a team player
- showing initiative
- having a customer focus
- paying attention to standards.

However, there are a number of other factors that will come into play when employers are considering your suitability for their organisation. These include:

- any personality traits considered to be helpful in a specific job
- whether your behaviour is consistent with a particular organisational culture
- whether you will work in a complementary way with others.

In these respects, there is no right or wrong type of personality. What is considered 'right' is simply what is suitable for that particular context. An example might be the mental toughness required to be a traffic warden or the patience of a care assistant, but certainly not vice versa.

# *Your personality*

There are many personality-type questionnaires, the most well-known of which is probably Myers-Briggs, which are used by employers to help them choose staff with the behavioural traits identified by the company as necessary for effective performance in a specific role. For instance, a company might want to check whether candidates for a trainee auditor role can work in a systematic and detailed way and bring an honest and professional scepticism to their work.

However, when we look at personality and behaviour from an individual's perspective rather than in relation to a specific role, we can see that there are some other factors that need to be considered.

> I hated my last job. My boss was very fussy about how he wanted things done and I used to get quite angry that he would make such a fuss over small details and it made me feel incompetent.    *Sian*

For instance, your workstyle may be broadly consistent across different jobs. If you are highly organised in one job you are likely to be equally organised in another. However, there may be many reasons why your behaviour might also change. For example, even the most socially confident extrovert may start behaving in an anxious and uncertain way if they are feeling undermined by others at work.

I'm sure there will be times when you remember feeling on top of the world in your job: bright, confident, energised and capable. However, most people have also had at least one miserable work experience when the things you thought you were good at seemed to evaporate.

> **TIP** We will revisit the exercises in this chapter when we create your Career Summary document on p245.

The following exercise is based on many of the personality 'types' indicated in the most commonly used personality questionnaires. For this exercise, deliberately look for consistencies in your workstyle across different work contexts, rather than just looking at your current role or any exceptions.

# Exercise 24: Self-assessment ⬇

24

1. Answer the questions below as honestly as you can. There are no right or wrong answers: the questions are merely prompts to get you thinking about you. The purpose of the exercise is simply to help you understand more about yourself at work.

2. Provide examples where you can as evidence for your answers. You can choose from different jobs or career-related experience as you wish, but your examples must be work-related, not personal.

3. Feel free to add any other personality traits or behaviours that you think are accurate for you.

|  | Answers and examples |
|---|---|
| Do you like working in detail or are you more of a 'big picture' person? |  |
| Are you a meticulous planner or are you more spontaneous? |  |
| How comfortable are you working in high-pressure situations? |  |
| Do you like to be the leader or the helper? |  |
| How have you handled any failures at work, either your own or others'? |  |
| How comfortable are you talking to people you don't know? |  |
| Do you like a set routine or do you welcome interruptions? |  |

*(Continued)*

| | |
|---|---|
| How competitive are you? | |
| Would others describe you as more of an optimist or a pessimist? | |
| Do you like things to be perfect or are you happy with 'good enough'? | |
| How creative or artistic are you? | |
| Do you like to blend in at work or do you enjoy being different? | |
| Which do you enjoy working with the most: facts and figures; abstract concepts; practical things; or people? | |
| Are you an original thinker? Do you like to look at new ways of doing things? | |
| Are you results-oriented or is the process as, or perhaps even more, important to you? | |
| Would other people see you as more of a 'doer', a 'thinker' or a 'people person'? | |
| If you manage staff, how would your staff describe your management style, for example consultative, commanding? | |
| Do you prefer working with things, equipment or hands-on tasks rather than intellectual or emotional challenges? | |

*(Continued)*

| | |
|---|---|
| How comfortable are you with taking risks? | |
| Do you like working as part of a group or team or more independently? | |
| How important is it for you that you are physically active in your work? | |
| Do you like helping or caring for people? | |
| Do you like working to targets and deadlines or do you prefer a looser structure? | |

## ⭐ Example

| | Answers and examples |
|---|---|
| Do you like working in detail or are you more of a 'big picture' person? | Big picture person. Enjoyed working on the new policies but preferred leading the discussion rather than writing the actual policies, which were cumbersome and a bit boring. |
| | When making a deal, I like building the relationship but I will leave others to manage the nitty gritty of the contract negotiation. |
| Are you a meticulous planner or are you more spontaneous? | I delegate a lot of the organisation to Maria who does it on my behalf. I just point her in the right direction. |
| | Wouldn't say I am a meticulous planner – can be a bit last minute, for example last year's conference, but it still tends to work out in the end. |

*(Continued)*

| Do you like a set routine or do you welcome interruptions? | I would get very bored if I did the same each day. Enjoy the variety. I like the unpredictability of my job, for example I think having to manage the product recall was something I did really well considering the time constraints we were under. |
| --- | --- |
| How comfortable are you working in high-pressure situations? | It was pretty stressful when we didn't know whether the company was being sold or not. I think it affected me only because it wasn't clear if I could make decisions or not. But normally I have to deal with lots of things that are pressured, for example trying to work out what went wrong with the product batch and handling the emergency recall. |
| | *Victoria* |

Your answers provide important clues to help you identify which roles and organisations might suit you best in the future.

For instance, there is no point working in a sales-related role if you don't like working to targets, regardless of how attractive the rest of the package may sound. If you are someone who needs to work in a quiet, focused way then a busy open-plan office is not where you are likely to do your best work.

American psychologist John L. Holland developed a careers inventory which is often used by career advisers to help individuals think about suitable careers based on their workstyle and the kinds of organisations that would be compatible.

The inventory outlined below consists of six factors and I've included a sample list of jobs which, although not exclusive to each factor, are likely to be complementary to that workstyle.

# ✸ Holland career inventory

| Factor | Suitable jobs |
|---|---|
| **Doer** | |
| Realistic, practical, physical, hands-on, tool-orientated, mechanically inclined | Chef, mechanic, paramedic, police officer, vet, chiropodist, occupational therapist, hairdresser, personal trainer, conference organiser |
| **Investigative** | |
| Thinker, analytical, intellectual, scientific, explorative | Lawyer, doctor, statistician, psychologist, business analyst, laboratory technician, marine biologist, software developer, market researcher, economist |
| **Creator** | |
| Artistic, creative, original, independent, chaotic, non-conforming | Writer, advertising consultant, designer, PR professional, marketing manager, inventor, photographer, musician, animator, film-maker |
| **Social** | |
| Helper, co-operative, supporting, helping, healing/nurturing | Nurse, therapist, charity worker, social worker, teacher, receptionist, mediator, customer service adviser, coach, aid worker |
| **Enterprising** | |
| Competitive environments, leadership, persuading, selling, dominating, status, persuader | Sales executive, retail professional, investment banker, management consultant, publisher, politician, journalist, estate agent, business strategist, entrepreneur |
| **Organiser** | |
| Conventional, detail-orientated, organised, attention to detail, status | Proofreader, technical writer, quality control officer, computer programmer, auditor, logistics professional, company secretary, accountant, town planner, clinical researcher |

*Based on the Holland Codes by John L. Holland*

# Exercise 25: Your personality type

1. Now that you have read through the Holland Career inventory, which type do you think is most like you and why?

2. Using your answers from Exercise 24, and the Holland Career inventory write down below which factor you think suits you the most. Don't worry if you want to write down more than one factor. Where you are a blend of types, then you'll be pleased to know that there are many jobs that could sit in both categories; for example, an engineer could be both practical and investigative, while a nurse might fit with both the realistic and social categories.

3. Where one factor is clearly more dominant, this inventory can be a helpful steer for the kinds of jobs to investigate.

My work personality

*(Continued)*

## Your team's style

Your compatibility with a specific role will also of course be influenced by the particular team, organisation and manager with whom you are working. Each organisation has its own culture and your manager will very much dictate how they want things done. For instance, if your manager is a stickler for detail, you will be required to work with high attention to detail regardless of whether the job function usually requires it or not.

It's also worth remembering that organisations also have their own distinctive personality. They will have a particular way of working, an expectation about what they think is the right way to do things and therefore what they demand of you.

Here are just a few examples of different types of organisational culture.

| Type of organisation | Explanation | Job example |
|---|---|---|
| Bureaucratic | Importance of following processes, rules, procedures, paperwork | Civil service |
| Altruistic | Focus on a higher value than monetary gain | Charity organisation |
| Entrepreneurial | Innovative, risk-taking, quick to act on opportunities, dynamic | Business start-up |
| Expert culture | Organisations where knowledge is prized | University or legal firm |
| Task culture | Project-based, action-oriented | Manufacturing, farming |
| Power culture | Organisations where decisions are made either by one person or a few key players | Family business |
| Creative | Where ideas, originality, aesthetics are important | Advertising, arts organisations |
| Reward culture | Where staff are rewarded for performance rather than length of service | Sales-driven organisations, the City |
| Strategic | Focused on longer-term objectives, research and development, planning | Think tanks, government departments |
| Short-term focus | Organisations where product or service has a short shelf life so speed is of the essence, or temporary organisations set up for a particular task | High-street fashion, crisis helplines |

# *Exercise 26: What suits you?*

Write down in the box below the type of organisation you think would most complement your workstyle.

You might also think about organisations where you have worked in the past that you loved or loathed and which organisational culture best describes them.

This information will be useful when you come to write your Career Action Plan on p227.

> **My preferred type of organisation**

Your personality and behaviour at work is such a key factor in your career success that it is important that we look at ways to validate your self-assessment.

The next chapter will help ensure that those self-perceptions match those of others who know you.

# 13  FEEDBACK

When you were compiling your history or looking at your world back in Chapter 3, you'll have discovered how subjective your world is. It can be very tricky to be completely objective and there is often a mismatch between how we see ourselves and how others see us. You may be full of doubts but other people may see a confident person. You may be worried that you are coming over as too pushy, when in fact others see someone who lacks assertiveness.

## *How others see you*

In your career you are constantly being judged on your capabilities, behaviours and personality, both in your current job and any new jobs you apply for. It is essential that you understand what other people can see. Sensitive though it can sometimes be, obtaining objective feedback from others is by far the best way to do this, and is one of the most vital elements of the career coaching process. It will help:

- build your confidence in the things you are good at
- verify what you believe you have to offer a potential employer
- provide additional information that you may have missed
- identify any shortfalls that may emerge
- advise on how you might bridge any gaps
- provide a benchmark for how you compare with others.

In order to do this, we are going to use a process commonly used in business called a '360-degree appraisal'. It is basically a feedback exercise where you choose people who know you to comment on what you do well in the workplace and what you could do better and see if they have any advice. Most people are only too happy to offer their opinion if asked. Their view will be a subjective one. People will see you in very different lights and know you under different circumstances. You only need to think about previous jobs that you either loved or hated to see that one would have brought out your best qualities, another the worst.

However, it is likely that there will be some common themes that come up again and again and which are likely to be part of a shared perception that other people have about you wherever you are. So let's find out what they are.

# Exercise 27: 360 degrees

The aim of this exercise is to obtain feedback from people you know about your positive skills and traits as well as the areas which need development.

**1.** Collect together any appraisal reports, feedback, work emails, etc. in which someone is giving you feedback on your work related performance, your behaviour or personal qualities. It doesn't matter whether you agree with it or not – just collect it together.

**2.** Write a list of people who you are comfortable to approach for feedback, and who have known you in a work context. This could include managers, colleagues, trainers, customers. Aim for a minimum of four people, with at least one being someone who has managed you or who is in a more senior position than you.

> **TIP** Choose people who you think will give honest but constructive feedback.

**3.** Explain that you are seeking personal feedback to help you in your career development and ask whether they would be willing to arrange a time to answer some questions. Ideally they will be prepared to meet with you to discuss this because these discussions are always better face to face. However, if they are not able to meet you, you can send them the questions by email or talk to them on the phone.

TIP You can also choose to ask family and friends the same questions. Although there will be differences in your work and home behaviours, they may have another interesting perspective, especially if you frequently have conversations with them about what is happening at work.

**4.** Ask them the following questions.

How would you describe me?

What do you think I'm good at?

What areas should I work on and why?

Have you any advice about what I could do to develop my career?

TIP You may also want to check if they agree with your self-assessments in Exercises 24, 25 and 26.

Make sure you completely understand what is being said, and ask for clarification if there is anything about which you are unsure. Ask them to give examples wherever they can of what you do well and the areas that require attention. Stay open-minded and if there is anything you feel is unfair, accept that this is their view rather than trying to persuade them otherwise.

## ✳ Example feedback: from your ex-manager

### How would you describe me?

Positives: Hard-working, conscientious, perfectionist, trustworthy, expert, reliable, clever, invaluable in a team, sets the standard, gets the job done.

Negatives: bit hard-going sometimes, serious, can be argumentative, sometimes inflexible, hard taskmaster, which can be demotivating, very challenging, likes things to be done in a particular way.

### What do you think I'm good at?

You are very detail-oriented. I can always expect your work to be done thoroughly and well, without mistakes, for example I've never had to make many corrections to your work so I feel I can trust you to get it right. Your work on the new website was excellent.

### What areas should I work on and why?

You are quite hard on yourself, which means you have very high expectations of yourself and others. This means that you can get disappointed and frustrated when things don't go according to plan. Managing your personal emotions when dealing with practical problems will help others see you as the problem-solver, rather than someone who seems overwhelmed – your frustration with the web development company meant we had to calm you down.

### Have you any advice on what I could do to develop my career?

Go for the ideal but also check out also what is the minimum requirement. You then give yourself room for manoeuvre rather than trapping yourself and others. Use more positive encouragement with others rather than language of fear, such as telling people where they are on track rather than just talking about how much they still have to do. Be positive about outcomes and proud of them rather than disappointed if it fell short of your ideal. If it works, it works.

*Pete*

5. Once you have gathered the information from all your feedback discussions, collate them together and summarise them all below or on a separate piece of paper.

What positive comments did you receive?

What do you need to work on and how will you do it?

Were there any surprises?

Are there any implications for what you or others see as your career capital or workstyle?

What else have you learned from this exercise?

## ⭐ Example

What positive comments did you receive?

Everyone thought I was a friendly person and well mannered. They thought that I could talk to anyone and was very charming. That I looked good and was very professional. They thought I was a very good representative for the company.

What do you need to work on and how will you do it?

Being more assertive with people who were problematic. Could be too eager to please – sometimes needed to say no earlier. Needed to be able to show a tougher edge if want to progress in career. Will talk to HR for advice.

Were there any surprises?

I thought my people skills were great but other people didn't feel that I was good at handling conflict. I think they are wrong but this is clearly a perception that more than one person had.

Are there any implications for what you or others see as your career capital?

There is a mismatch at the moment until I can prove that I can handle conflict and be decisive.

What else have you learned from this exercise?

That being likeable isn't enough. I need to demonstrate toughness. So I need to look out for opportunities to do that.

*Emma*

**TIP** We will revisit this exercise when we create your Career Summary document on p245.

We saw in Part 1 how important our self-perceptions are in terms of our career. In this chapter we have confronted how far those perceptions match those of others. Feedback will be useful throughout your career to ensure you are on the right track and advise you how to get to your destination even more quickly. You just need to ask!

## Looking at your workstyle

In Part 4 we have looked at your workstyle and the type of organisation that might suit you best, and sought feedback from others to provide different perspectives that may have supported or even challenged some of your self-perceptions.

This will help you enormously when you come to set your career goals and when you are looking for a career move.

**28**

## Exercise 28: Reflecting on Part 4

Review the following exercises:

- Exercise 24: Self-assessment
- Exercise 25: Your personality type
- Exercise 26: What suits you?
- Exercise 27: 360 degrees

Now let's take a moment to capture any other thoughts, ideas or information that have surfaced. Think about the following, for example.

- What has been helpful to you in this section?
- What emotions have you felt while working on this section and why?
- Any other comments.
- Any actions to be taken.

## ✳ My reflections on my personality and workstyle

## ✳ Action points

## ⍟ Example

> I was taken aback by the feedback exercise. While there were some things I knew, for example that I was a very task-orientated person and great at getting the job done, I hadn't realised that people saw me as quite so ruthless. I don't suffer fools gladly and I guess that is why I have always been very comfortable working in quite aggressive commercial organisations. I think a slow-paced organisation or 'ditherers' would drive me nuts. Got some good useful advice, I think, about my need to move from a 'cracking the whip' style to a more leadership approach, especially if I want to move into more strategic roles.

## ⍟ Example: action points

> 1. Ask HR if they can arrange coaching or mentoring for me to develop my people management expertise
> 2. Pay more attention at work to building good relationships
> 3. Next career move must be in a fast-paced, commercial organisation
>
> *Simon*

> **TIP** We will revisit this reflections exercise when we look back on your career coaching journey in Exercise 48, p250.

Well done for all your hard work so far – we've come a long way. You've examined your career from every angle, from both current and historical perspectives, internally and externally, with a microscope and with 360-degree panoramic vision. Along the way you will have begun to collect together elements of your Career Action Plan.

You should now have very firm bearings from which to confidently start planning your future career journey.

# Options and decisions

## PART 5

From here onwards, the career coaching is going to be very future-focused as we start to look at your options and make decisions.

However, you may have found that some positive changes have already started to take place. You may have spoken to your boss, arranged some personal development or started applying for a new role. You may have had a meeting with a business contact that resulted in a job interview or made some decisions about the future.

Whether or not things have already started to change for you, the career management strategies in this section will show you how to make good career decisions and achieve your career goals.

## In this section we will:

✓ **visualise what you would like your future to be**

✓ **understand your options**

✓ **generate job ideas**

✓ **thoroughly reality-check your options**

✓ **make a career decision.**

# 14 SEE THE FUTURE

I n this chapter you are going to create a clear picture in your head of what you want your career to look like.

This is especially important if you feel, as many people do, that your future career seems 'vague' or 'fuzzy'. If you don't know what you are looking for, then how are you going to find it?

I speak to lots of individuals in this situation who describe feeling stuck because they 'don't know what it is out there'. They have been wearily trawling through recruitment adverts looking for inspiration and then been disappointed when they don't find it. Their CV will be unfocused because they are trying to cover too many job options, and when they speak to recruiters, their doubts will spark questions about their suitability as a candidate. The perfect job for them might well be under their nose but they wouldn't recognise it.

Their error has been in looking outwards for inspiration, when the decision-making needs to start off by looking inwards. This chapter is going to help you do just that.

## Exercise 29: Career wish list

29

1. Before completing this exercise, take another look at the exercises in Part 1, especially Exercise 6 (p35). Look at the things you wanted to change when we first set out on this career coaching process.
   • Are those career desires still as current for you?
   • Do you have any new priorities?

2. From the list below, highlight which are your current career priorities. Feel free to add as many others as you wish.

3. Refer to your key career 'I wants' from Exercise 6.

| | | |
|---|---|---|
| More money | Adventure | Greater appreciation |
| Increased responsibility | Security | Improved relationships |
| Greater recognition | More respect | Greater job interest |
| Work with new people | Greater challenge | Move sector |
| Promotion | More confidence | See my kids more often |
| Greater job interest | More people contact | Retrain in new area |
| More decision-making | Less people contact | Ensure skills in demand |
| Intellectual stimulation | Greater variety | Stop working long hours |
| Learning opportunities | Progression | Less pressure |
| Less stress | To feel that I'm 'growing' | Play to my strengths |
| More fun | Easier travel to work | To be really good at my |
| Greater status | More flexibility | job |
| To make a difference | Gain experience | To prove I can do it |
| Greater reward | Deepen expertise | To find a new job after |
| New environment | Improve employability | redundancy |
| More freedom | Set up own business | To return to work after a |
| More travel | Use creativity | career break |
| More perks | Use entrepreneurial skills | To pay the bills |
| Better work/life balance | Less hours | To feel proud |

# Using visualisations

We are now going to use this career wish list as a basis on which to visualise your ideal career. Remember how powerful the picture was in Chapter 2, when you drew your world as you saw it today.

> Visualising your goal as if it has already happened triggers feelings of motivation. It helps us to become focused on the end result and so acts like a magnet pulling us towards our goal. *Avy Joseph, City Minds*

Visualisations are helpful not only in bringing to the forefront important psychological information that may be hidden or unexpressed; they can also help you create the future.

How can they do this? Imagining a situation and how you will deal with it can be self-fulfilling. Visualising yourself in a specific set of circumstances is like

> I use my visualisation before I go to a networking meeting. It reminds me of myself at my best and what I am trying to achieve. **John**

a rehearsal for a play. You've already mentally arrived. You know what to do and, what's more, you start acting as though you are already there. Your mind is following the neural pathways that you have set down.

In career coaching, creative visualisations have a number of benefits. Being able to see what it is you want and describe it makes it easier to articulate to others. This fact alone can make the difference between achieving the changes you want and staying stuck where you are.

Positive visualisations can also be very helpful preparation for challenging interactions such as job interviews, networking meetings, presentations or a difficult conversation with the boss. Your psychological approach will have a huge influence on any interactions you have with others at work.

In the following exercise, we are going to use a career visualisation that embodies your hopes, needs and aspirations and can act as a meaningful touchstone for making important decisions about your career goals.

# Exercise 30: Visualising the future

**30**

1. Read the instructions below and then close your eyes and try and blank out the world and any distractions around you. You will need to spend a minimum of 20 minutes on this exercise.

2. Think about your wish list in Exercise 29. Now imagine waking up on your perfect day at work. Visualise your whole day from the time you get up in the morning to the moment when your head rests on the pillow at night. You might want to include the following details.
   - How do you feel when you wake up? What does breakfast look like? Is there anyone else around? What do you choose to wear? How do you get to work and what is the journey like?

- At work, what activities are you involved in? What are your interactions with other people? What have you achieved in the morning? What do you do for lunch? What do you do in the afternoon?
- What do you do after work? What is your journey home like? What happens when you get home?

3. Create all the sights, sounds, smells and feelings associated with your perfect day at work. Immerse yourself imaginatively in the picture and enjoy every single detail. This picture is you at your best and most positive.

4. Did that feel good? Now let's make your visualisation tangible by drawing a picture on p137 of the key elements you saw and the emotions you felt. Remember, your drawing skills are completely unimportant. Try to use colour in your drawing to help your creativity flow. You can use the odd word if you need to.

## ✳ *Your picture*

## ⚹ *About your picture*

**Use your visualisations and pictures to draw out the following.**

What are the most important elements of your career vision for you?

What are you doing?

What emotions are involved?

Who else is in the picture and what is your relationship with them?

What are the key differences from your world now?

What real-life things do you need to do to make your picture a reality?

*Example*

## ✳ Example

> What are the most important elements of your career vision for you?
>
> Seemed to be busy but relaxed and it felt like the work was under control.
>
> That I was working between home and the office – and avoiding the rush hour commute. That I wasn't being bombarded with interruptions like I normally am.
>
> What are you doing?
>
> I was involved in meeting customers and suppliers rather than just behind the computer.
>
> What emotions were involved?
>
> Felt the calmness, lack of hassle both from boss and commuting.
>
> Who else is in the picture and what is your relationship with them?
>
> Had brief images of being interrupted by my boss which made me feel angry but then it calmed down again. Was talking to customers.
>
> What are the key differences from your world as it is now?
>
> - Better journey into work or more flexi-working.
> - Being able to get on with my job without interruptions.
> - Being trusted to represent the company with customers, etc.
>
> What real-life things can you do to make your picture a reality?
>
> - Could talk with my boss about staggering my start times at work.
> - Need to manage interruptions at work more effectively.
> - Find a new job nearer to home or home-based.
> - Volunteer to go to exhibitions and trade events.
>
> *Jane*

It is really important for you to keep hold of your vision and replay it in your head regularly, keeping it fresh and always positive. The more you practise it, the sharper the vision will become. It will help keep you focused, motivated and resilient, especially if things get tough.

> **TIP** Having the image on easy recall will make it easy to express clearly to others what you are like when you are at your best and what it is that you are looking for.

# 15 WHAT ARE MY OPTIONS?

Now you've got a clear idea of what you'd like your future to look like, we need to start thinking practically.

In this chapter we will look at the options available to you and get you to start thinking about which is the most likely route to the career vision you imagined in the last chapter.

The great news is that everyone has options! There will be opportunities right under your nose as well as further afield. There will be some that you can step right into and others that you may need to inch towards. However, whatever your career issue or circumstances may be, you have a number of choices.

Broadly speaking, there are the following options.

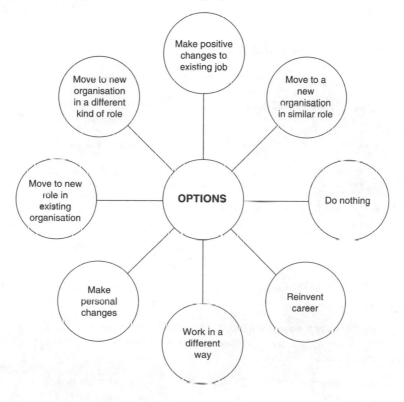

Let's look at each option in turn.

# *Do nothing*

Of course, this is an option. The fact that you bought this book implies that you want something to change, and that doing nothing at all is perhaps not your favoured option.

I really don't like my job. I feel sick on Sunday evening just thinking about going into work the next day and I spend most of the week just waiting for the weekend. But that's just how work is, isn't it? It's not like it would be any better elsewhere, not in today's job market.      *Helen*

Nonetheless it remains a choice that is open to you. Let's look at the pros and cons of this.

## ✳ Pros and cons of doing nothing

| Pros | Cons |
|------|------|
| Takes little effort to do nothing | May take enormous effort/stress to continue status quo |
| It might not be the right timing | Life is too short for regrets |
| Others around you may not want change | Others may prefer to see you happy and fulfilled |
| Things could change of their own accord | Being proactive increases the likelihood of getting what you want |
| Low risk? | May be risks to staying where you are |
| Threat to financial security | Limits on potential financial gain if you stay put |
| Low self-esteem says that it's your fault and you don't deserve anything better | Well-being improves as a result of a move to a healthier environment |
| Doing nothing avoids risk of failure or rejection | Doing nothing means that others may take the opportunities I want |

If this is an option that you are leaning to, it might also be worth looking again at Part 2. Have the positive things that have happened to you career-wise been a result of things just landing fortuitously in your lap or have you made them happen?

There can be an argument sometimes for doing nothing. It may be that if you sit tight that elusive promotion opportunity at work will finally appear or the threatened redundancy won't happen. However, while many people see 'doing nothing' as the safe option, it is in fact the most risky, because it reduces your options.

# *Make positive changes in your current role*

This is an option that is often overlooked, mainly because people are often nervous about what they see as rocking the boat with their current employer. However, there are lots of ways in which you may be able to enhance or modify your current job to more closely match what you need, and sometimes a subtle change can make a big difference. You could, for instance:

- talk to your manager and/or HR about your career development
- ask for opportunities that stretch your capabilities
- request a pay rise
- make sure you get credit or recognition for your work
- talk to your boss if the workload is too much
- be more assertive with your manager and/or colleagues
- manage your time more efficiently
- write a blog, organise an event or join a project group
- spend some time with other departments
- undertake in-house training or train others
- take control over your work/life balance
- ask for a coach or mentor – or mentor someone else.

Remember that it is in an employer's interest to keep their current staff motivated and engaged as they are more likely to perform better at work. Good staff are hard to find and expensive to recruit and train, so it makes financial sense for an employer to make an effort to retain the staff they want to keep.

> I asked my manager what I could do to improve my promotion prospects and she was very supportive and suggested that I need to get some budget management experience so we agreed that I would spend an afternoon with the finance department. I've now been delegated the monthly accounts and I feel much more confident. My manager has also started delegating me other things now that she knows I want to progress my career, so I feel like I'm learning again. *Linda*

However, if you are asking for something that requires additional resources, do make sure that you can show how the organisation will benefit, if you want them to agree to it. For instance, they are unlikely to fund an expensive management development course if it is not relevant to your job or they think you will leave as soon as you have completed it. They will want to see a return on their investment.

## Take on other opportunities in your organisation

This may include actively seeking a promotion, a secondment, a sideways shift or even a down-shift in terms of your responsibilities. There are many advantages to this.

> I was fed up working as a retail floor manager and thinking about changing career entirely. When the training job at Head Office came along, I pulled out all the stops to make sure I got it. I now feel like I've got my motivation back. **Tim**

- Familiarity with the organisation means that an internal move is relatively low-risk compared with an external move.

- Your legal continuity of service and accrued employee rights are preserved.
- You are already likely to have some relationships in place that will help you.
- You can fully explore what the job entails before you accept.
- It looks good on your CV to show that you have been entrusted with different roles within the organisation, especially if they are promotions.
- You can try new things and develop your capabilities but within the comfort of a known environment.
- If you have been with your employer for a long time, exposure to different roles in the organisation will help your employability.
- It can be a stepping stone that takes you closer to an external role that you would otherwise be unable to step straight into.

**TIP** If you are looking for a job move, it is always worth exploring what may be available internally. Too often employees hand in their notice without even considering what might be on offer.

# Look for a new role outside your organisation

There may be lots of good reasons why you are looking externally for your next role. They could include:

- threat of redundancy
- limited opportunities
- unhappy workplace relationships
- boredom or disenchantment
- appeal of a fresh challenge
- being underpaid
- wanting to use different skills and expertise
- feeling unrecognised or undervalued
- being overworked
- poor management
- wanting a new career direction
- changes in personal circumstances.

You may decide to look for a similar role, something allied to what you have been doing, or a complete career reinvention. It is very important that you are clear about what you want in a new role, otherwise there is a danger that you drift into something similar or are squeezed into something that is not right for you at all.

> I was going from sales account job to sales account job moaning about my job and the people and just generally being really frustrated, fed up and cynical about work. It was only when I took a step back and considered that, although sales was the only thing I had ever done, I really didn't enjoy working in that highly pressured sales environment. I took a job instead in customer relationship management and immediately felt more comfortable and have done really well ever since. Why didn't I work that out earlier?
>
> *Sophia*

147

If you have had several unhappy work experiences, you might have to face the fact that you may be contributing to this. It might be a result of faulty choices, a mismatch in expectations or that your interpersonal skills need development.

In which case, it is better to sort out these issues rather than assume that the next job might be better – it probably won't. Working on your personal development, maybe with a career coach or counsellor, could be of far more help than simply changing jobs.

# Work in a different way

You may want to continue using your core skills, experience and knowledge, but deliver them in a different way. Options include:

- changing your working hours
- working in a job share
- having a portfolio career where you work in a number of different roles
- doing voluntary work
- combining work and study
- working from home
- working seasonally, or just in term-time
- working on a project basis or in temporary positions.

If you are looking to make changes in *how* you work, for example working in a job share, you need to make sure that the new arrangement is logistically workable not just for you, but also for the employer. You might, for example, argue that a job share ensures that someone is available to cover the job during the holiday periods when you are away. But if the employer can't see how it is going to work in their favour, they are likely to say no.

# Portfolio career

Having a portfolio career means your working week consists of different jobs. Your jobs may be similar in terms of their content or they could be completely different. A portfolio career might include a couple of part-time jobs, ad hoc projects, running your own business or unpaid roles.

I've worked with many clients with interesting combinations. Some have combined consultancy, writing, lecturing and unpaid advisory roles in the course of their working

> I work as a teaching assistant during the day. I'm also a gym coach, secretary to a local committee and organise local nearly-new sales for toddler and baby toys. **Julie**

week. Others have had one job in the day and another completely different one in the evenings and at weekends. This included one client who was such an adept multi-tasker that his working week including working in corporate sales, running his own profitable e-commerce site and regularly undertaking ambitious property redevelopment projects.

Portfolio careers can be an excellent choice for those who:

- enjoy lots of variety in their working life
- like the independence of not being tied to one employer
- want to work part-time and need flexibility, such as mums returning to work
- are not interested in a corporate career, including those who want to continue working after retirement
- can use portfolio working as a stepping stone to a new career or to building their own business
- cannot find a job that brings together all their particular interests and skills in one role.

However, portfolio working requires a great deal of organisation. It can be tricky to co-ordinate and each employer will want full value in terms of your time and effort. To work successfully, you will need to put clear boundaries around each job. For instance, if you are paid by the hour for one job, you need to make sure that you are not on the phone to one of your other employers during that time. Only good jugglers should consider portfolio work.

## *Interim or temporary work*

Another alternative way of working is taking temporary or interim work. Temporary work can cover a whole array of different working arrangements including opportunities arranged through an agency, directly with an employer or on a consultancy basis.

If you are interested in working for a particular organisation but struggling to be considered, temporary work can be a great way to gain entry. I've coached many graduates who have successfully used temporary work to get their foot in the door and then ended up with a permanent job.

Working temporarily in a job can also give you valuable experience that you might need to apply for your next permanent job. For instance, public sector workers looking to transfer to the private sector can use temporary work to help them in that transition.

Interim roles are usually undertaken by senior managers or subject specialists. They are brought into an organisation to complete a specific task or provide cover for a member of staff who is temporarily absent. Examples might include an organisational development consultant delivering a change management programme or a finance manager covering the post-holder's maternity leave.

Interim work is well worth considering if you like working in a variety of different settings and being able to pick and choose your assignments. Many professional interim roles pay more per day than their permanent employee equivalents but there is far less job security and fewer employee rights. Some interim roles will require you to set up your own company so that you can supply your services on a 'contractor' basis.

> **TIP** The short-term and task-focused basis of interim work means that it is particularly suited to those who are goal-orientated and who can hit the ground running on day one of their assignment rather than needing time to settle in.

Many people enjoy the variety and flexibility of working in interim and temporary roles and have built successful and well-paid careers. However, in a tough economic climate, the interim and temporary job markets become more competitive than usual because many people who fail to get permanent work consider this as an option.

# *Reinvent your career*

It is highly unlikely that your first job will be the same one from which you retire. Most people will have several career changes during their life. Sometimes a career change evolves naturally as your growing interest in an area finds opportunities in which to express itself. At other times it may be triggered by a redundancy, a health scare, a new baby, a milestone birthday or a change in personal circumstances, which may lead you to re-evaluate what you want for the rest of your working life.

A career reinvention can take many forms, including:

- becoming more specialist in a particular area
- broadening your expertise to become more generalist
- becoming involved in advising, recruitment, training, coaching or quality control within your field
- writing about your subject area or working for relevant bodies, like a trade union
- using your transferable skills in a new role or sector
- retraining for a completely new career
- actively pursuing a new area of work that interests you, such as charity campaigning
- turning a hobby into a profession, for example garden design.

The ease with which you will be able to reinvent your career is likely to depend on how close the new role is to what you have been doing before. If there are gaps, it is worth considering stepping-stone roles which will edge you closer over time to where you want to be.

Career change is at its most challenging for those who are mid-career and who may need to retrain and/or take a salary drop. In this instance, you need to consider very carefully whether this is financially viable for you and how likely it is that a prospective employer will hire a 'mature novice' in this field. Even with age discrimination legislation, late entrants to some professions, for example medicine or law, will find it more difficult at a later stage of life. However, there are some career change options where 'life experience' is a positive advantage, such as coaching, consultancy or training.

# Self-employment

The option to work for yourself may be appealing to you. There are a number of different ways you can go about this – from going freelance providing a service to starting your own business from scratch. Below are a few ideas.

- Work freelance as a sole trader, marketing and delivering your services directly to potential customers or working as a sub-contractor for other companies.
- Create a business to sell a service or product.
- Take over an existing business.
- Buy a franchise and run your own business under an established brand.

> **TIP** For more information about starting a business, go to www.startups.co.uk. For more information about franchises, check out the British Franchise Association at www.thebfa.org.

Self-employment can be very rewarding. However, any new business venture brings a different set of challenges from those of being an employee.

While it offers much greater independence and potentially greater rewards, running your own business is riskier, more pressured and is likely to take you into areas that are outside your comfort zone. For instance, regardless of your particular expertise, you are going to have to become involved in selling. No product or service just sells itself. If you don't have a sales background, acquiring these skills can be quite a steep learning curve. You will also have to deal with issues that as an employee you had other people to do for you: accounts, invoicing, VAT, IT systems, marketing, premises management, legislation ... the list goes on!

Yet many people (including myself!), once they have started their own business, never want to go back.

There are resources on p260 for those who want to find out more about self-employment.

# Make other personal changes

As we've found already, your career does not exist in isolation from the rest of your life. It may be that there are changes that you can make outside of the workplace that could have a positive impact on your career. Examples could include:

- changing childcare arrangements to something that works better
- asking for more support from your partner
- taking up a creative hobby to express yourself outside work
- leaving earlier to miss the traffic
- updating your image to change perceptions at work.

You may remember that we looked at some of these practicalities in Chapter 3 on work/life balance. Your answers to Exercise 3 (p21) will form one of your career goals in your Career Action Plan (p227).

As you can see from this chapter, there are lots of options for you to consider, so let's capture your initial thoughts about which are the most appealing to you.

# Exercise 31: Interesting options

**31**

1. Think of your career wish list (Exercise 29, p133), and your future career picture (Exercise 30, p135).

2. Consider all the options in this chapter and feel free to bring in any others you think are relevant. Which options do you think offer the best route to achieving your career vision?

3. Are there options which can act as useful stepping stones to get you closer even if they don't take you the whole way?

4. If you are currently working, could there be any possibilities within your current organisation?

5. Write your answers on the next page.

OPTIONS

## ✳ *Example*

> Definitely interested in looking outside my organisation for a new role.
> Not sure yet whether it should be allied to what I am doing currently
> or moving it a step closer to more project type work. Also interested
> in portfolio work and maybe setting up own business.
>
> I could try and get myself on some project groups to build my
> experience. This would definitely help if I wanted to focus more in this
> area in the future. I can talk to my manager about that because it will
> seem really keen and he will probably like that.
>
> Interested in doing a role that is more project management based
> Definitely want a role that is a promotion from where I am now – so
> could stay in same sector but just go for a step up. Am kind of
> interested in interim work – although not sure I am ready for that yet.
>
> **Meera**

In this chapter we've covered a lot of options available to you, many of
which could help you on your way to your next career move and your longer-
term career strategy.

At this point, if you have a good idea of exactly what you want your next
role to be, you can go straight to Chapter 17 to look at reality-testing.

However, if you are unsure about what job you want, perhaps because you
are considering a career reinvention, the next chapter is going to help you
generate lots of job ideas for you to consider.

# 16 GENERATING IDEAS

We have already looked in depth at your career capital and also your workstyle, so you are likely to have a sense of what you are good at, what you enjoy and the way you like to work. We've also looked at the many options you could consider, one of these being to move jobs.

This chapter will help you generate more ideas for potential jobs, if you are thinking about moving sectors or roles, by showing you where you can start looking for new jobs and opportunities.

> **TIP** Generating ideas can take time, so enjoy your research and take this opportunity to delve into areas you may not have considered before.

## *Careers information resources*

There are so many potential fields for you to choose from that sometimes it can feel a bit daunting. The list below indicates the main headings for more than 750 different job profiles that are available for you to look at on the website www.nextstep.direct.gov.uk.

Administrative and Clerical
Alternative Therapies
Animals, Plants and Land
Arts, Crafts and Design
Catering Services
Construction

Education and Training
Environmental Sciences
Financial Services
General and Personal Services
Information Management
Information Technology

Legal Services
Maintenance, Service and Repair
Management and Planning
Manufacturing and Engineering
Marketing, Selling and Advertising
Medical Technology
Medicine and Nursing
Performing Arts, Broadcast and Media

Publishing and Journalism
Retail Sales and Customer Service
Science and Research
Security and Uniformed Services
Social Services
Sport, Leisure and Tourism
Storage, Disputching and Delivery
Transport

Pick the ones which are of interest to you and then find out more detailed information on the different roles available in these fields.

Other websites with helpful careers information include www.monster.co.uk, which features Careers Snapshots for over 2,500 jobs with links to related vacancies.

The graduate careers site www.prospects.ac.uk also offers careers information including career ideas for those studying for different degrees.

> **TIP** Don't get too stuck on job titles as these can vary widely. Focus more on the main activities of the role and the type of organisation or sector.

# Interesting organisations

If there is a particular organisation or type of organisation that appeals to you, for example management consultancy or a charity, go directly to relevant company websites to find out more about the type of positions they have.

> **TIP** Many larger companies have a careers section on their website with lots of useful information including vacancies, job descriptions, organisation charts and case studies. For example, www.bbc.co.uk/careers includes articles and videos about different roles, entry schemes and vacancies in the BBC.

The company may also have a social media site on Facebook or LinkedIn where you can find out more about the company, get regular information updates and participate in online discussions.

Once you start looking at organisations that appeal, you will discover the different capacities in which they employ people. You can then decide whether any of them are job roles that you would be interested in pursuing further.

If you know anyone who works for the organisation, ask them to keep you updated if any opportunities arise.

## Ask people you know

Share with people the key elements of your career capital and your career vision. Talk about your practical skills and experience and then describe, from your career picture, the type of work activities and organisations you are interested in for the future. Ask them for their suggestions. Encourage as many contributions as you can – family, friends, contacts, colleagues. Reject nothing at this stage. Other people can have great ideas or spark some new ideas of your own.

## Use the newspapers

I kept highlighting jobs that were animal related because I love my dogs. My background is IT so I wasn't going to retrain to be a vet but it did make me think that I could work for an organisation that was animal related. I'm now working in IT for a big animal welfare charity and loving it.          *Ian*

Look through the papers (both national and local) and highlight any jobs that sound of interest. It doesn't matter what the job title is or how unrealistic they may be. Consider what it is about each of these jobs that appeals to you. For instance, if you like a job because it has an international component, this will give you a steer to look for roles consistent with your existing background but which have an international dimension.

> **TIP** Job fairs are held across the country and throughout the year and these are worth attending as they give you the opportunity to talk directly to the recruitment teams from many different organisations and find out more about the opportunities that are available.

# Recruitment sites

There are thousands of different possibilities listed on recruitment websites. While there's probably too much information to start trawling through randomly looking for career inspiration, the key word search function on each database can be very helpful.

For example, you might be interested in marketing but also music. Type in several keyword combinations adding any relevant filters such as salary range or location and see what the database comes up with as a suitable job. It's like a keyword job lucky dip and is great for generating job ideas. If you find something you like, use the job title to explore other jobs in the same field.

If you know that you want to find out more about the range of roles within a specialist function, try websites operating exclusively in the relevant niche area.

> **TIP** Some newspapers have extensive online job listings, so remember to take a look at these as well e.g. www.telegraph.co.uk.

# Online forums and resources

There are many online forums where you can participate in career discussions. This might be Facebook or LinkedIn groups, professional networks or community discussion portals like those at www.netmums.co.uk for women who want to return to work.

The *Guardian* careers website at www.careers.guardian.co.uk features not only articles, but also videos and podcasts on a whole range of career-related matters. It also offers regular interactive online Q&A forums with industry experts advising on what it is like to work in a particular field and how to get your foot in the door.

Take advantage of these forums to generate and test career possibilities.

> **TIP** Don't forget about the library, where there will be books and directories providing a wide range of career and occupational information and signposts to local initiatives, like careers services and any job-seeking support groups.

# Exercise 32: Your ideas

1. Spontaneously write down below all the job ideas which interest you – aim for a minimum of six. They may be ideas that you have been thinking of for a while, prompted by this chapter and your investigations, or suggested by other people.

2. Capture your ideas as a mind-map as in the example, or as a list or diagram.

3. Don't exclude anything at this stage.

4. From your list, decide which ones are the most appealing. Circle these or highlight them, and start with these when it comes to the next stage of your research – in Chapter 17.

✳ *Example*

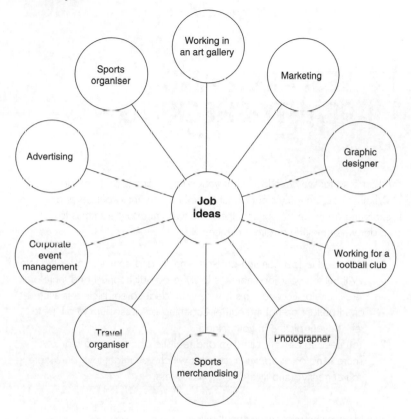

---

**TIP** If you are still finding it difficult to either generate ideas or to process the information available, you will find it helpful to talk to a careers professional such as a career coach or careers adviser. They can signpost you to relevant career ideas and help you gauge their suitability.

# 17 RESEARCH AND REALITY-CHECKING

In Part 5 so far we have looked at your career options and job ideas. Whether you are fairly clear about the role you want to pursue or are exploring a number of options, there are two important elements to consider when making a career choice.

1.  You need to feel genuine passion, energy and enthusiasm for the role. Without this your job search is likely to be half-hearted and therefore less likely to succeed. This is why your ideal career picture is such an important part of the career coaching process. (Turn to p137 to refresh your picture in your mind.)
2.  You need to be very clued-up and realistic about the job market. There is no point applying for roles which you might love but where you currently stand little chance of success.

> I would have thought twice about being a sound engineer if I'd realised what working freelance involved. There is no security. I'm having to work away from home all the time. It's not what I wanted.      *Ben*

Even if the job you want is currently out of reach, don't be disheartened. If you are not ready to jump into it yet, look for a stepping-stone role that will take you closer. Perhaps undertaking some additional training or obtaining some more experience would help you get there quicker. Alternatively, there may be another career route which will give you what you want career-wise, but be easier to achieve. There is no point making it more difficult than it has to be.

In this chapter we are going to look at the options and ideas that interest you and then reality-check them, because you need to know that what you are aiming for is realistic.

# Beware assumptions!

Many clients come to career coaching because they have been disappointed at the lack of success in their job applications. Very often it's because they have simply misunderstood the employer's requirements and are applying for roles for which they are unsuitable. For instance, I have talked to several people who believe that because they were a manager in one organisation they can be a manager in *any* organisation. While management is a transferable skill, it does not in itself necessarily make you the right candidate for every management job. There will be a whole range of other selection criteria that you will need to satisfy.

If you have been surprised to be rejected for a job for which you thought you were the ideal candidate, the chances are that

> How could they not interview me? I had everything they wanted. It's ridiculous!
>
> ***Charlotte***

your application made some false assumptions about what you thought the employer wanted to hear.

It is essential that you do your research properly rather than making short-cut assumptions as it will save you an awful lot of time, energy and frustration later when you come to implement your Career Action Plan.

# What you need to find out

Whether you are fairly clear about your next move or considering a number of options, you must research the following.

- The market demand for this type of role, now and for the future.
- Typical entry routes into the job and progression opportunities.
- Qualifications and training requirements.
- What the job involves on a day-to-day basis.

- Salary information.
- Selection criteria used by employers to recruit candidates.
- Feedback from recruiters/employers on your suitability.
- Information about organisations that recruit for these roles.
- Inside information from those who currently work in the role or organisation in which you are interested.
- Any personal factors or circumstances that could help or hinder in this role.

# How to access this information

## ✳ Job market demand

When you are making any choice about your next career move, you must check out the likely job market demand.

Some jobs and sectors are predicted to grow, such as healthcare and homecare services as a result of the ageing population. Others are in decline, for example record shops, as consumers turn to digital downloads.

Do not rely on recruitment websites alone to try to assess the demand. You may see lots of relevant jobs listed on a website and make the assumption that the job market is healthy. However, it is not unusual for the same job to be advertised several times on websites but labelled differently. Some job adverts are also 'teasers' to attract candidates to sign up with a particular agency rather than being an actual job. You need a much more accurate picture of employer demand.

The UK's Sector Skills Councils are independent, employer-led organisations which analyse the job market trends in different sectors. Check out these sector reports to find out the trends for the specific industries and types of job you are interested in. You need to know whether demand is likely to be strong or whether the market is already saturated with good candidates and the longer-term prospects doubtful. A full list of all the Sector Skills Councils can be found on pp255–257.

See also specialist recruitment websites and professional associations which feature analyses of job market trends in their respective professional areas. For example, www.brandrepublic.com contains information on careers in advertising, marketing, media and PR.

## ⭐ Using job ads

You may feel you have looked at hundreds of job ads during your research in Chapter 16. But there is a skill to reading them properly and getting as much information out of them as possible.

# Exercise 33: Interpreting job ads ⬇

**33**

1. Find three to four job adverts for **each** of the kind of roles you are interested in applying for.

2. Look very closely at the job details from the different job ads you have gathered together and answer the following questions for each role option.

## ⭐ Role option 1

What activities do the jobs have in common?

Is the job what you expected it to be?

What are the differences between the jobs?

Which is more appealing to you and why?

What are the selection criteria? Are you a good match?

*(Continued)*

Are there any gaps? If so, is there anything you can do to bridge them?

## ✴ *Role option 2*

What activities do the jobs have in common?

Is the job what you expected it to be?

What are the differences between the jobs?

Which is more appealing to you and why?

What are the selection criteria? Are you a good match?

Are there any gaps? If so, is there anything you can do to bridge them?

## ⚁ Example

### Sample job advert

Job title: Charity Fundraiser

This role involves:

- developing the major donor/corporate fundraising strategic plan
- delivery and implementation of that plan against targets
- producing leaflets, reports, films for donor meetings
- soliciting large donations (£25,000+) and developing the patron programme
- liaising with patrons, organising events, receptions, briefings, discussions, etc.
- identifying new prospects from our databases and outside sources.

Person specification:

- five years' fundraising experience, including at least three in major donor fundraising or client liaison experience
- proven track record in developing major donor relationships
- demonstrable strategic and creative approach to developing fundraising opportunities
- experience of making outstanding presentations, networking, negotiation and influencing others
- excellent interpersonal skills and the ability to communicate, both orally and in writing, at all levels
- proven events experience

---

What activities do the jobs have in common?

Devising campaign plans and organisation, meeting donation targets, events organisation, donor relationships.

Is the job what you expected it to be?

Mostly. Lots of emphasis on finding new prospects.

What are the differences between the jobs?

Some are more focused on individual patrons, others looking for corporate donors or government/lottery support. Jobs seemed to be quite different depending on who they were approaching for money.

*(Continued)*

**Which is more appealing to you and why?**

I think I would feel more comfortable working with corporate donors as this is more my background. I understand what organisations are looking for in terms of their corporate social responsibility aims.

**What are the selection criteria? Are you a good match?**

I match quite a few of the things they are looking for. Particularly the events organisation, making presentations, writing leaflets and other communications. I think I have great experience in this and I have done this for charities before. However, I haven't worked specifically in fundraising.

**Are there any gaps? If so, is there anything you can do to bridge them?**

I don't have the substantial experience of working solely in fundraising. However, I think I would be very good at it. If I could find myself a role working as an assistant in a fundraising department I could learn how to devise and organise a fundraising campaign plan and I think I would very quickly prove myself.

*Barbara*

If you can satisfy a minimum of 95% of the criteria on the job ad and provide examples to prove it, this is likely to be a good match. Although, of course, this may depend on how important the missing 5% is to the employer. If there are any gaps, you will need to come up with a very good argument as to how they will be bridged, if you want to be considered.

Should you find that the role isn't quite what you expected or you don't match what they are looking for, it may be that this role isn't for you – or at least not yet. It may be that it is part of a longer-term strategy that you can work towards.

## Salary research

Unless you are independently wealthy, it's important to know the market rates for the types of job you are interested in. There's lots of good salary information available online. Simply type into your internet search engine the keywords 'salary survey' along with your chosen job title or sector, and you will find a variety of different reports. I've also included a list of useful salary survey websites on p257.

However, before you get too carried away looking at the top end of the salary ranges, bear in mind that it's a tough job market out there, with plenty of good candidates on the market. If employers are spoilt for choice they have little incentive to pay premium rates.

> **TIP** It's important to know the likely salary range for a job before you apply for it. If it's not listed, ring up the recruiter and ask. They'll usually tell you as there is no point in wasting either your or their time if it's not suitable.

In addition, recruiters want to know your current or previous salary to determine your level of seniority. If there is too big a jump between what you have been earning and the salary in the new role, they may simply consider that you are too junior.

## ✳ Talk to people ⬇

Inside information from people who are currently in the role or who hire for the role is invaluable. Seek out anyone who can give you the answers to the following questions and write their answers down.

- What does a typical day in this type of role involve?
- What are employers looking for when they recruit for this role?
- What differentiates the people who are good at this job?
- Do you think I'm suitable?
- What is the future demand for these types of role?
- What advice can you give me in applying for these roles?
- Will you let me know if you hear of suitable opportunities?

> **TIP** Use your existing contacts but also be proactive: go and talk to those who have the information you need. You can also use online forums: LinkedIn is a great place to connect with people from a certain sector.

## ✳ Work tasters

See if you can spend some time with someone who currently works in the role you are interested in. This might be a work placement, a voluntary assignment or even an unrelated temporary job in the department where you want to work. You will get an insight into the day-to-day reality of the job. You can also add it as relevant experience on your CV and use it as an opportunity to network and get advice while you are there.

> **TIP** The research in this chapter is likely to take you several hours, days or even weeks. Diligent research now will save you plenty of time further downstream.

Once you have completed as much research as you can, gather together the findings of your research below.

## *Exercise 34: Job research summary* ⬇

1. Answer the following questions for every role you have been considering. You may need to continue on another piece of paper.

---

What is a typical job title for this type of role?


What have you found out about the role?


How well does the role match your current skills and experience?


Are there any gaps between what you have to offer and what recruiters want? If so, how can you make up the gap?

---

*(Continued)*

What is the salary range?

How do people normally get into this role?

What are the advantages of this as a career choice for you?

Are there any disadvantages?

Does it take you closer to achieving your career visualisation? If so, how?

Is it a good fit for you as a career choice? If so, why?

## ✳ Example

> **What is a typical job title for this kind of role?**
>
> Online marketing assistant.
>
> **What have you found out about the role?**
>
> That it involves a mixture of technical and creative skills. Lots of time spent in front of the computer so very static. Very results driven. It needs lots of energy, writing skills and coming up with new ideas. It is very analytical as you need to keep a close eye on statistics and fine-tune what you are doing. Also about relationship building and brand building.
>
> **How well does the role match your current skills and experience?**
>
> My marketing degree will stand me in good stead. I understand the psychology of talking to customers. My strong visual creativity will also help in creating aesthetically pleasing and eye-catching content. I have very good IT skills.
>
> **Are there gaps between what you have to offer and what recruiters want? If so, how can you make up the gap?**
>
> Experience in search engine optimisation (SEO) and social media, which I have little experience of. I can read up all about SEO and using social media for business. I can also offer to help my current employer with their SEO, getting them listed in free directories, investigating pay per click campaigns. I can also talk to a couple of my friends who work in this area to find out more about what is involved.
>
> **What is the salary range?**
>
> Between £15k and £25k for first or second job in this area.
>
> **How do people normally get into this role?**
>
> Trainee role. Usually an IT/marketing background. Or they already work in the organisation and they take over responsibility for this as one of their duties.
>
> **What are the advantages of this as a career choice for you?**
>
> Great use of my marketing degree and IT skills. If I can find a role in which I can also use my creativity, e.g. sports or visual arts, then this would be ideal.

*(Continued)*

**Are there any disadvantages?**

No. Only that I am going to have to work hard to show that I am capable. May need to take a pay cut to get in at entry level but it will be worth it.

**Does it take you closer to achieving your career picture? If so, how?**

I think the combination of IT and creativity will give me the job satisfaction I really wanted – and that was the biggest factor in my picture – my feeling that I could express myself at work.

**Is it a good fit for you as a career choice? If so, why?**

Yes, it is a really good use of my degree and uses a lot of my skills. I am sure that I could do well in this role.

*Louis*

2. Once you have done this, are your choices about your next career move becoming clearer? Is there one option that has become a clear favourite or are there two or three which still appeal?

3. Write down below the job option(s) that you would like to take forward to the next stage.

My preferred option(s)

1.

2.

3.

# 18 MAKING A DECISION

Now you've got your options, this chapter is about helping you make smart decisions. We are going to use the research you've collected about you and your job choices to make sure that your next move is one that will give you what you are looking for career-wise.

> You've got a lot of choices. If getting out of bed in the morning is a chore and you're not smiling on a regular basis, try another choice. **Steven D. Woodhull**

Whether you have made your career decision or are still considering a few options, let's put some of your career ideas through their paces to find out whether they are realistic and robust.

There are a number of different exercises in this chapter to help you in making your decisions.

## Seven tips for effective career decision-making

### 1. Do your research

Gather together all the information and facts you need to help you make that decision. These may include written materials, opinions, statistics, advertisements and internet research. You should have lots of this from Chapters 16 and 17.

## ✲ 2. Listen to your intuition

If the facts say one thing but your gut instinct is telling you another, the mismatch is trying to tell you something. Work out what it is and whether it is valid or not.

## ✲ 3. Enjoy making decisions

Treat your career decision-making as an enjoyable research project. If you feel under pressure or are impatient to make a quick decision, slow down, or you could miss some important information that may hold you back later on.

## ✲ 4. Talk out loud

Many people find that talking through their options or decision with someone else is very helpful. So if you need to, find someone who is a good listener to help you.

## ✲ 5. Don't catastrophise

There are very few things in life that are irreversible. Build in a review period once the decision has been made, and if you've given it all you've got and it's not working, try something else.

## ✲ 6. Manage risk

Every decision – including the decision to do nothing – has an element of risk. Accept that even with the best information in the world, you can't possibly know everything, cover every eventuality or guarantee success. However, if your career decision entails considerable financial risk, make sure you have a fall-back plan just in case.

## ✲ 7. Commit to your decision

Once you have made your decision, put all your energy behind it in order to make it work. The right decision executed half-heartedly is more likely to fail than the wrong decision implemented with gusto.

## *Considering your options*

You may remember that right at the beginning of the coaching process we looked at the pros and cons of your current career situation (p33). We are now going to do the same for your career options to make sure that you are taking as objective a view as you can.

## *Exercise 35: Pros and cons*

1.  Write down below, or on a separate piece of paper, the advantages and disadvantages of each option you are considering.

2.  Make notes, including any implications, queries or conditions that may apply.

| Pros | Cons | Notes |
|------|------|-------|
|      |      |       |

## ✴ Example

**Becoming a history teacher**

| Pros | Cons | Notes |
|------|------|-------|
| Like working with kids | Need for substantial retraining | |
| Works around family life better than current job | May still need to arrange childcare depending on location of school... | Can probably come to an arrangement |
| Could work more locally | No guarantee would find a local job | |
| Personal interest in the subject | Not all the kids may be interested | |
| Fits with my values of making a difference | Would I find the organisation a bit slow compared with the fast pace of where I've been? | |
| More scope for creativity than in my current job | Lots of bureaucracy to deal with which I may find frustrating | Friend who is a teacher has been telling me about all the paperwork |
| Regular income | Drop in salary | |

It may be that at this stage one option is coming out as a clear favourite. However, if there are a few that still seem equally attractive, the next exercise will help you weigh up the options in more detail.

# Exercise 36: Decision-making ⬇ worksheet

**36**

If there are a number of options you are considering, try the following comparison worksheet to help you choose. The example on p180 shows you how it works.

1. Think of your career wish list and career picture (Exercises 29 and 30). List up to 10 of your career priorities for the future and rank them in terms of their importance to you, making the most important priority number 10 and the least important number 1.

2. Insert the options you are considering, e.g. staying where you are, starting your own business, moving to a similar job in a new company.

3. In the Probability column, decide how likely it is that this option will satisfy the priorities that are important to you: 10 means that it is very probable and 1 is unlikely. Your market research will be useful here.

4. Multiply the Career Priorities Ranking number by the Probability number and enter it into the subtotal column for that option. Then add the subtotal scores up for each option at the bottom of the column to show how each option compares in respect of meeting your career requirements.

> **TIP** You can download this form as a spreadsheet by going to our website www.personalcareermanagement.com/careercoach.

> **TIP** Feel free to adjust the priorities and weighting if needed and play around with different options. See p180 for an example.

| Career Priorities | Career Priorities Ranking (1–10) | Option 1 | | Option 2 | | Option 3 | |
|---|---|---|---|---|---|---|---|
| | | Probability | Subtotal | Probability | Subtotal | Probability | Subtotal |
| | | | | | | | |
| | | | | | | | |
| | | | | | | | |
| | | | | | | | |
| | | | | | | | |
| | | | | | | | |
| | | | | | | | |
| Total | | | | | | | |

## ★ *Example*

| Career Priorities | Career Priorities Ranking (1–10) | Option 1 Move to similar job in new organisation | | Option 2 Stay where I am | | Option 3 Retrain as teacher | |
|---|---|---|---|---|---|---|---|
| | | Probability | Subtotal | Probability | Subtotal | Probability | Subtotal |
| More money | 10 | 5 | 50 | 1 | 10 | 1 | 10 |
| Promotion opportunities | 9 | 4 | 36 | 1 | 9 | 1 | 9 |
| Recognition for my work | 8 | 5 | 40 | 1 | 8 | 2 | 16 |
| Security | 7 | 1 | 7 | 5 | 35 | 6 | 42 |
| More responsibility | 6 | 5 | 30 | 1 | 6 | 4 | 24 |
| Work in a sector that is growing not contracting | 5 | 6 | 30 | 1 | 5 | 5 | 25 |
| Good journey into work | 4 | 7 | 28 | 7 | 28 | 9 | 36 |
| Offers leadership training and development | 3 | 4 | 12 | 2 | 6 | 5 | 15 |
| To feel at end of day that I have made a difference | 2 | 5 | 10 | 1 | 2 | 8 | 16 |
| To have good bunch of people to work with | 1 | 4 | 4 | 4 | 4 | 5 | 5 |
| **Total** | | | 247 | | 113 | | 198 |

You can see from the example that moving into a similar role in a new organisation emerges as the preferred option in this instance.

If you are at all uncertain that the option that emerged from Exercise 36 is the right one for you, double-check by completing the following decision-making exercise.

## Final check

Very often when we make decisions, we use a preferred decision making style. We may choose an analytical approach or tend to rely on 'gut feelings'.

> Both optimists and pessimists contribute to our society. The optimist invents the airplane and the pessimist the parachute.                   *Gil Stern*

Optimists may underestimate difficulties or assume they don't need a contingency plan because everything is just going to work out fine. On the other hand, pessimists can get so wrapped up in the pitfalls they miss the boat.

The following exercise forces you to move outside your normal thinking and decision-making style to obtain a more balanced view.

# Exercise 37: Decision perspectives

Take your preferred option and test it thoroughly from all perspectives. Answer all questions below, and write down your answers.

**Facts**
Do you have all the information you need?

What factual evidence do you have that this option is realistic?

Have other people confirmed that this option is realistic?

**Emotions**
What emotion(s) do you feel when thinking about this option?

What does this reaction tell you about the option you have chosen?

How do you think others will react emotionally to this career decision?

**Negatives**
What are the downsides to this option?

Why might it not work?

What would happen if this option didn't work out?

*(Continued)*

**Positives**
What appeals to you about this option?

What could it mean for you if you succeed?

How might others benefit if you succeed?

**Creativity**
If you had complete freedom, what would you do?

Did you generate lots of different ideas before making your decision?

Are there any other routes you could take?

**Systems**
What processes need to be in place for this option to work?

How will you know if this option is working or not?

Who and what will keep you on track?

## ✴ *Example*

### Facts

I have looked at my finances and all the study options and decided to do a distance learning course because I can work at the same time. I will ask work to support me because I can argue that it is in line with my job, but I'm prepared to fund it myself it they don't. I have spoken with recruiters and they have told me that it would definitely be an advantage to me if I had this qualification. I have also spoken to two people who work in this field who have told me the same.

### Emotions

I feel apprehensive about investing this money and the fact that it is going to be tough to find the time in the evenings and at weekends to do the work. However, I feel very focused that this is the right thing to do. I feel relieved that the qualification will give me more credibility whereas in the past sometimes I felt like I have been winging it. My partner will be very supportive but might get a bit fed up that a lot of my free time will be taken up with the course.

### Negatives

My time is going to be in very short supply, stretched between work, studying and home life. I might fail the course or not complete it. However, as the course is flexible learning, I can always take a break between modules if it's all getting too much. The worst thing would be if I spent all this time and energy on the course and then stayed where I was in my job. Must make sure that doesn't happen.

### Positives

Am genuinely interested in the subject. I am looking forward to becoming qualified. I like the fact that this is something I have wanted to do for ages. If I succeed in moving into a new job in this area then I will feel very happy. It fits with what I want from my career, my job satisfaction I think will greatly increase as well as my opportunities to progress further. I think also people will be really proud of me.

### Creativity

I would definitely still want to do the course but I would start applying for jobs now rather than waiting to finish studying. I wonder if I could

*(Continued)*

apply for jobs telling them that I am about to start studying? There is nothing to stop me joining the networking groups at the institute and LinkedIn to start making connections. I could also talk to those guys I met at the exhibition. The other route I could take is to move to an organisation that specialises in this area and make an internal move.

## Systems

My time management needs to improve as I'm going to be juggling work, home and study and looking for a new job. Probably need to allocate set days to do homework. Also will need to make special time for partner to keep relationship sweet. Perhaps I should plan out my diary in advance. Because the course is in complete modules, I can review at the end of each module how it is going, take a breather and then plan for the next one. Alongside studying I will need to keep an eye on any suitable job opportunities – don't want to miss anything because I'm too busy.

*Charlie*

# Exercise 38: Career decision-making checklist

**38**

Before you finally make your decision about your career options and goals, let's make sure you can tick off all of the following items in your decision-making checklist.

| You have... | Yes |
|---|---|
| Considered different options before making your decision | ☐ |
| Researched exactly what the role involves | ☐ |
| Talked to people who work in the field | ☐ |
| Looked at job adverts for similar roles | ☐ |
| Identified any gaps and how to fill them | ☐ |
| Checked likely salary levels | ☐ |
| Talked to recruiters/employers who hire for these roles | ☐ |
| Considered any personal factors that might have an impact | ☐ |
| Weighed up both the advantages and disadvantages of this option | ☐ |

# Exercise 39: My career decision: what is my goal?

We have looked at your options, researched and then evaluated them to help you decide on your next career move and your career objectives.

We have also rigorously tested your preferred option to make sure that, as far as we can tell, it is realistic and workable for you.

Some options you have considered will be immediate goals, while some may be longer-term. These are important to bear in mind and will be incorporated into the Career Action Plan we will be developing together in Part 7.

If you are clear on your decision, write it down. Include both your immediate and longer-term goals.

I decide to:

### ✳ *Example*

I decide to:

- start my course even if I have to fund it myself
- use the course to increase my employability in this field
- make time for my partner while I am studying
- increase my specialisation in this field so I become an industry expert
- look for a new job in this sector.

*Nick*

**TIP** This exercise will help you fill out your career goals on p230, and you will be revisiting it when you compile your Career Action Plan in Chapter 22.

# *Looking back on your decision*

In Part 5 we have looked in detail at your options, generated job ideas and helped you make good and balanced decisions. It has been the point at which your self-research, your knowledge and understanding of your career capital and aspirations have come face to face with the realities of the job market.

This can sometimes be both confidence-building and uncomfortable in equal measure. It is incredibly motivating when you can find roles which play to your strengths and career drivers. However, sometimes this is coupled with the realisation that this is where the practical challenges begin.

If for any reason you are still unclear about your career decision, it might be that you just need to do some more research. Alternatively, it might be what is called a 'career block'. This could be related to some internal resistance you are experiencing, perhaps as a result of confidence issues, or a practical 'career block' that you just can't see your way round at the moment, such as a financial issue. We will be looking specifically at these blocks in Chapter 19. If this sounds like you, you might find it helpful to read ahead and then come back to this section again.

> **TIP** If you are really struggling with any aspect of the career coaching process, don't beat yourself up – just ask for help! Whether it is talking it over with a good friend or seeking specialist careers help, don't stay stuck – do something about getting the help you need.

If you still find it difficult to decide, I would suggest that you try talking to a career coach or a careers adviser. A careers adviser will be an excellent information resource and signpost you to helpful resources. They usually offer one-off appointments or telephone discussions. A career coach will normally be someone who works with you in more depth, over a longer period of time, helping you with your self-research, looking at options, addressing career blocks and helping you with the job search practicalities. For more information, turn to p254.

However, if you think your issues may be more psychologically deep-rooted, then there are some useful self-help resources listed at the end of the book which may be more appropriate for you.

## Exercise 40: Reflecting on Part 5

Review the following exercises:

- Exercise 29: Career wish list (p133)
- Exercise 30: Visualising the future (p135)
- Exercise 31: Interesting options (p153)
- Exercise 32: Your ideas (p160)
- Exercise 33: Interpreting job ads (p165)
- Exercise 34: Job research summary (p170)
- Exercise 35: Pros and cons (p176)
- Exercise 36: Decision-making worksheet (p177)
- Exercise 37: Decision perspectives (p182)
- Exercise 38: Career decision-making checklist (p185)
- Exercise 39: My career decision: what is my goal? (p186)

Let's take a few moments to capture any other thoughts, ideas or information that have surfaced. These might include the following.

- What has been helpful to you in this section?
- Were you surprised at your decision or is it what you expected?

- What emotions have you felt while working on this section and why?
- Any other comments.
- Any actions you want to take.

## ✷ *My reflections on my options and decisions*

## ✷ *Action points*

## ✲ Example: my reflections on my options and decisions

I felt frustrated that I couldn't step right into the job I wanted. Recruiters simply did not feel that I had the experience needed and that I was wasting my time applying. This was a bit of a blow but at least it explains why I'm not getting shortlisted.

I am going to have to approach it in steps rather than making the big leap I hoped. A couple of people told me that they thought I should try to get into the right type of organisation and try to achieve a sideways move from within. This is how they did it, so I am going to try this. However, my research came up with a couple of other suggestions that are also interesting and perhaps easier for me to achieve, so I am going to look at both options in tandem.

## ✲ Example: action points

1. Identify the roles I could apply for that would give me a way into the organisations I want to work for.
2. Find out from my contacts which organisations tend to be more flexible in how they deploy their staff.
3. Continue researching some of my other career ideas.

*Aseem*

**TIP** We will revisit this reflections exercise when we look back on your career coaching journey in Exercise 48, p250.

# Making it happen

Now that you are clear about where you are heading career-wise, it is time to move on to the action stage.

This section is devoted to the career management strategies that will help you achieve your career decision. It provides resources to help you, and flags up some of the potential obstacles you may need to overcome.

## In this section we will:

✓ **remove obstacles to career progression**

✓ **look at who can help you in your career**

✓ **perfect the art of self-promotion**

✓ **give you tips on your CV and interview technique.**

# 19 WHAT MIGHT GET IN THE WAY?

Let's face it: if it was easy for people to make the changes in their career that would make them happy, the job satisfaction ratings for employees in the UK wouldn't be so low. A 2011 survey by Monster.co.uk reported that a whopping 73% of 2,500 people were unhappy in their current role.

So let's also take a moment to anticipate some of the challenges you might face along the way.

There are some common problems that people face when trying to make changes in their career or working life. These 'career blocks' tend to fall into two categories.

1. **External blocks.** These are very practical and tangible. An example might be a gap in your qualifications or experience required to get you on the shortlist for the job you want. It could also include real personal constraints such as your availability to work, or family commitments that restrict your ability to travel.
2. **Internal blocks.** These are more psychological in nature but they can be powerful enough to scupper even the best laid career plans. They may be rooted in issues like poor self-esteem, fear of losing control, or discomfort with risk. These anxieties may have developed relatively recently but they can often be traced back to earlier life.

It is very common for individuals to confuse what might be an internal block with an external one, and vice versa. An indication that an internal block might be holding you back is when a perfectly reasonable solution to an 'external block' is consistently met with a 'Yes, but...'

# The most common career blocks

This isn't a comprehensive list, but below are some of the more common blocks that surface, in my experience of working with career coaching clients.

**External blocks**
Financial pressures
Insufficient time
Strong competition
Lack of information
Discrimination
Location
Family commitments
Lack of required skills or
  qualifications
Lack of connections
Problematic career history
Insufficient experience
Social pressure
Poor health

**Internal blocks**
Lack of focus
Poor confidence
Fear of change or loss
Poor energy or motivation
Anxiety
Poor assertiveness
Fear of failure or rejection
Pessimism
Conflict avoidance
Overly tolerant
Introverted or shy with people
Unable to make a decision
Too cautious or distrustful
Too spontaneous

## 41

# Exercise 41: What are your career blocks?

1.  Write down below all the things you think could get in the way of achieving your career goals.

2.  Use the above list as a prompt, but you may also find it helpful to ask these questions about your career progress to date.
    *   What problems have you come up against in the past?
    *   What, if anything, do you think might have held you back?
    *   What difficulties do you see for the future?

> Things that might get in the way of achieving my career goals:

## ⚝ Example

> Things that might get in the way of achieving my career goals:
>
> • Finding enough time to do this – am exhausted when I come home.
> • Don't like dealing with rejection.
> • Find the job search process stressful.

When you name your concerns or frustrations, we can then start to look at practical ways to overcome them.

> **TIP** We will revisit this exercise when we create your Career Summary document on p245.

# Tackling common career blocks
## ⚝ I'm worried that if I try, I will fail and look stupid

Most people will have some understanding of this block. No one likes to fail or look stupid. In itself this isn't a problem – in fact it's a great incentive to do everything you can to succeed. However, if 'the fear of failure' is the big black cloud that is keeping you stuck where you are, then let's look at your worst fear head on, to see whether in fact failure deserves its negative reputation.

> I was the biggest failure I knew... It is impossible to live without failing at something, unless you live so cautiously that you might as well not have lived at all – in which case, you fail by default.
>
> *J. K. Rowling*

Are there actually any advantages to having tried and failed? Without the experience of failure, you would not be able to:

- learn from your mistakes – know how to do it better next time
- understand where the gaps are
- reality-check your expectations
- know what contingency plan you need next time
- ask others for help and advice on what you now know are the problem areas
- avoid regrets for missed opportunities.

## WHO WOULD HAVE THOUGHT?

- Jamie Oliver – left school with two GCSEs
- Richard Branson – poor academic record due to dyslexia
- Simon Cowell – bankrupt at 30 and living with his parents
- Bill Gates – university drop-out
- Michael Jordan – dropped from high school basketball team for 'lack of skill'
- Steven Spielberg – rejected three times by University of Southern California film school.

In most cases, people's fear of failure is disproportionate to the actual effect a real failure would have. If you were unsuccessful in applying for a promotion or a new job, what would happen? Not a lot – you continue as before. If you made a job move but it didn't work out, what would you do? Get yourself another job as soon as you could and move on.

You should also avoid the assumption that staying where you are is always a safer option. This is not always the case. If there are threats to your job or you are under stress, it could be far riskier to do nothing, both to your job prospects and your health. If you think that this might be an issue for you, go back to p33, where we discuss the pros and cons of doing nothing about your job situation.

### ✳ *I would love to, but I don't have the confidence*

Whether you want to ask your boss for career development, or impress a potential new employer at interview, appearing to have confidence in your own abilities is a prerequisite for other people taking you seriously.

> If you think you can do a thing or think you can't do a thing, you're right.
>
> **Henry Ford**

However, there are very few people who would say privately that they are entirely free of self-doubts. I coach many highly successful people who would appear to the outside world to be brimming over with confidence, but who, like most other people, frequently question whether they are 'good enough'.

In this respect, it is not the fact that you have self-doubts that is important. That is part of human nature. What matters is whether you let them hold you back.

I recently worked with a highly capable senior manager who had been made redundant along with many of her colleagues. She was someone who had very low self-esteem, but in her organisation she was very highly thought of and had been promoted. She ascribed her rise through the ranks to being 'so worried they were going to find out that I was rubbish that I worked harder than anyone else to keep them from finding out'.

Facing redundancy could have been her worst nightmare come true, given her usual state of anxiety. However, within a week she had two good job offers. 'I was so scared that I was never going to work again that I went absolutely hell for leather to find a new job. I didn't waste a moment – ringing everyone, getting my CV sorted, pulling in favours, networking like mad. I'm lucky it worked!'

Of course, it wasn't luck. She is a classic example of someone who has very little personal confidence but who had been able to use her fear and pessimism as a motivator to take action.

If you feel that your lack of confidence is getting in the way, you can try some of the following ideas to give you a boost.

> Even if you are on the right track, you'll get run over if you just sit there. **Will Rogers**

## Building your self-confidence

1. Think of your past successes. Review Part 3 to remind yourself of past achievements, your skills and abilities. Write down all the nice things that people have said about you.
2. Spend time with positive people who are supportive, encouraging and have your best interests at heart. Avoid whingers who just want you to moan with them.
3. Remember your picture of your ideal working day (p137). Create the picture in your head as vividly as you can. Revert back to this picture regularly to keep you on track.

4.  If your confidence issues are acute, talk to your GP or a counsellor about clinical help or talking therapies that may be able to help.
5.  Exercise and eat healthily. Exercise increases those feel-good endorphins and clears the mind. Yoga, meditation or even just going for a walk can help you work off nervous energy and reduce anxiety.
6.  Refresh your image. A new haircut and outfit that is smart and contemporary can give a real boost to your confidence.
7.  Experiment with new ideas or approaches in a safe environment. For instance, if you want to practise your networking skills, start with family and friends, graduating to other people you know and then to complete strangers.

> **TIP** Remember that the fear of doing something is usually far worse than the reality. Try it. You'll survive!

### ✳ I'd love to make a career move but I just can't afford to

This career block can take a number of forms, including:

- expecting that the career move will mean a drop in salary
- worrying about the financial risks of changing the status quo
- not being able to afford the training required for the new role
- waiting for a bonus or redundancy payment before moving
- not having the financial resources to set up on your own
- believing job satisfaction is a luxury and unrealistic.

If you are worried about the financial implications of taking a new role, it is very important that your concerns are built on accurate information rather than perception. Sit down and look at your personal finances to establish your financial needs and any flexibility you might have. Take some financial advice if necessary. We often spend according to our budget rather than our needs, so be clear about what your salary essentials are, rather than basing your assumptions on your current salary. Also, bear in mind the longer term: could there be greater earning potential for the future with this new role? Are there other benefits, such as a pension scheme, or could it perhaps mean a quicker, cheaper journey for you into work?

Is there a stepping-stone role you could take in the right direction, which would be close enough to your current position to attract a similar salary package? This is often a very workable solution. For instance, I remember working with a lawyer who was desperate to leave the legal profession and go into business, but who was worried about a drop in salary. He moved to a business consultancy role where his legal background was a huge asset because the organisation's principal customers were legal firms.

If the new role requires you to undertake costly training or a vocational course, investigate whether there are other less costly routes, perhaps a shorter course or on-the-job training. Could you do the training as part of an evening course so that you can continue to bring an income during the day? Can you get a student loan to help you pay for the course?

> **TIP** See p260 for websites where you can find out about courses.

In the event that your job is under threat from redundancy, check out the size of any potential redundancy payment. It may be less than you think, especially if you are only entitled to statutory redundancy monies. In which case it may be better for you to move into a new job as soon as you can, rather than risk a gap in employment when your job ends.

> **TIP** Check out www.acas.org.uk for details of your statutory redundancy entitlements.

And if you would love to set up your own business, the only way you are going to know whether or not you can afford it is to devise a proper business plan so you know exactly what your commitments and risks would be. On p260 there are a number of resources you will find helpful if you are considering self-employment.

You can see from the above that there are lots of things you can do to overcome a 'block' connected with financial feasibility. It may still turn out to be unrealistic for you. However, a word of warning. The 'financial' block is often presented by individuals as an external block when sometimes it has more to do with internal factors, like the individual's fear of change.

> **TIP** Make sure you have done your calculations thoroughly and counted the opportunity costs of staying where you are before deciding whether a job move is financially feasible for you or not.

## ✳ I just don't have the time to focus on my career – I'm too busy doing my job

If you are currently working, it's understandable that at the end of a hard day you may just want to relax. You might also have the dinner to make, the kids' homework to help with, or the gym to visit. In fact there are a million and one other things that you could be doing rather than investing time in making your career work. But, like anything else in life, you get out what you put in, and if you want something enough – no matter what it is – **you make the time!**

Smart time management is especially critical if you are currently working in a role that is demanding. You must continue to do a good job for your employer, while freeing yourself up some time to work on furthering your career plan.

Below are some ideas which can make your time management more effective and reduce the potency of that age-old excuse, 'I haven't got time'.

- Make a time schedule – see your Career Action Plan exercise in Chapter 22. Set yourself tasks and target dates for completion – and stick to them.
- Allocate specific times to work on your career, for example set aside Monday evenings to research, send off emails and work on your CV.
- Delegate what you can and decide what can wait. The house may need cleaning but in the same time you could have sent off several job applications. Defer routine tasks or shorten them, but don't use them as an excuse.
- Use your lunch breaks effectively, to meet with people, or ring up prospective employers.
- Stop staying late at work – leave work on time. Don't send or respond to emails at weekends or in the evenings unless they are urgent.
- Generate opportunities at work which will be developmental for you and beneficial to the company, such as spending time building relationships with customers and suppliers who could in the future become your new employer.
- Volunteer to help out at exhibitions and conferences where you can get to meet other people in your industry.

> **TIP** The Your Career Action Plan exercise in Chapter 22 has a schedule which you can use to set yourself tasks and target dates for completion.

At a time when people are working longer and harder than ever before, it can be tricky to find the time you need. However, you can always find the time if you are motivated to do so.

If you find yourself saying 'Yes, but...', be honest. It's not the time management that is constraining you; it's something else. Work out what it really is – you can then start tackling the real issue not the pretend one.

## ✳ I don't have the information I need

We live in a time when our access to information is unrivalled. The internet is a vast information resource and you have only to type keywords into your computer or even your phone to find out about career opportunities, specific jobs, training courses, job-hunting strategies and market trends.

There are many ways to access information, outlined in Chapter 17 – go back and make sure you have researched these fully. It will take time and effort to carry out the research you need, so expect it to require hard work. You may also need to accept that even with the best information in the world, you can't possibly know everything. You may just need to take a view and make your best guess.

It may be that your concerns are not about a lack of information at all, but relate more to an internal career block such as risk aversion. Consider what is going on for you emotionally as the difficulty may lie here.

## ✳ I know what I want to do, but I don't have the skills, qualifications or experience I need to compete with others already working in this area

First, make sure you investigate exactly what you need, rather than making assumptions. Look again at Chapter 17 to ensure that you have done all the research and reality-checking necessary to come to that conclusion. You could also do the following.

- Find the post-holders of jobs you are interested in on LinkedIn and look through their previous career history to see how they got there.
- Ask people who currently work in the field whether they know of anyone who came into the post from an alternative route.

- If you need a particular qualification for the role, make arrangements to start studying for it and say on your CV that this is what you are doing. This will show your commitment to your chosen career path and help reassure any potential employer that you will be able to bridge an important shortfall.
- If you can persuade your current employer that the skills and qualification would be of benefit in your current job, they may be willing to sponsor your training.
- Arrange to shadow someone. This could be a formal arrangement through work or an informal arrangement that you have organised yourself. Either way, it gives you relevant content to talk about on your CV and at interview.
- Consider voluntary work to plug some of the gaps. Being a member of the PTA or a governor at a school, joining a charity committee or organising a fundraising event can offer opportunities for you to extend your people management skills and project management abilities, and deepen your understanding of budget management, strategy development and organisational communications.

> I wanted to move from a technical role to a managerial one but had no experience of managing staff or strategy. I joined a management committee of a local training college and got involved in all kinds of issues from recruitment to devising strategy, governance and financial issues. It was fantastic learning. My company were so impressed that I had done this on my own initiative that they put me on the fast-track promotion panel for a managerial career. They loved my initiative and thought that that in itself was sufficient evidence of my management capabilities. *John*

If you have truly investigated all of the above and it is still evident that you don't stand a chance, you can:

- consider a stepping-stone role that may be similar to what you are already doing, but enables you to work in an organisation or sector that is more relevant to your target role. From there you can plot your next move to get even closer
- accept that the role is beyond your reach and focus on one that is more achievable.

## ✳ I've family responsibilities and I'm not sure that I can put my career first

If your current role complements your home life, enabling you to pay the bills, offering security, convenience and a reasonable work/life balance, then you may decide that while your current job isn't perfect, you are better off staying where you are. And you might be right.

However, there could still be other opportunities out there that might be even better. If you don't even look, then how are you to know?

For instance, going for a promotion does not automatically mean that you will have less family time. Often, the more senior you are, the more freedom you have to schedule your own diary. It can be easier to take the time off to attend the school play if you are a manager than if you are an assistant.

If you are in an uncomfortable situation at work, it is essential that you start trying to do something about it.

I remember talking to a guy who worked for a manager who was an absolute bully. He was making his life hell. However, he said that he felt he couldn't move because he needed the regular money his role brought in

What he didn't seem to have factored in is that no one - least of all his family – wanted him to stay in that situation. He was highly employable. What had happened was that his confidence had gone, he was highly stressed and he had lost faith in himself and his ability to go and find another job – so he wasn't even trying. His plan was to keep his head low, grit his teeth and bear it. What a grim prospect for anyone – knowing that the longer he stayed there, the lower his confidence would sink.

> **TIP** If you feel you are being harassed or bullied at work, contact either www.direct.gov.uk or www.mind.org.uk.

There is never any harm in looking around for jobs, networking, trying to create opportunities. Even if you get offered a job, you don't have to accept it if you don't feel it is right for you. But unless you start looking you will never know whether there is a role that might suit your current family circumstances better than your existing situation.

## ✳ My age is against me – that is why I am not getting shortlisted

Discrimination exists. It is often subtle and hard to prove, but there are undoubtedly some cases where individuals are rejected because of some prejudice of the recruiter.

At a seminar I ran recently, I asked 'Who feels their age is against them in looking for a new job?' Every single person in the room put their hand up, from the 18-year-old through to the 65-year-old. In fact most clients I have ever worked with have expressed the fear that they thought their age was against them.

However, in my experience, many people who feel they have been discriminated against – whether on the grounds of age, sex, race or disability – have actually been rejected because of other concerns with their CV or career history.

I recently spoke with a 30-year-old woman who felt that she wasn't getting interviews because employers probably thought that she was going to go off and have babies. Well, possibly – but when I looked at her CV, it was far more likely to be the spelling mistakes that were putting off prospective employers than her age.

With regard to age, it is, of course, true that some industries are more youth-orientated than others. Organisations specialising in social media and web design, for instance, tend to have younger staff. Clearly if you walk into an organisation where most of the people are considerably younger than you, it's going to be harder to make it look as though you fit in. However, on the whole, people will hire you for the contribution you can make to their organisation. Show them how you can add value and your age becomes irrelevant.

If you are not landing jobs for which you know you are suitable, then you need to a take a hard look at your applications and get some honest feedback. Is it your age? Or have you really shown that you can deliver what the employer is looking for?

> **TIP** Try the *You're Hired!* series of books published by Trotman (see p255) for advice on how to get yourself shortlisted for jobs.

Make sure your applications are as good as they can be and that you address head-on any potentially discriminatory misconceptions by the employer. For instance if you are a more mature worker, ensure that your CV comes over as high-energy, that you show how up-to-date you are, that you have learned new skills, and that you have recent achievements. This is the best way to address discrimination – by making the best darn application you can.

Bear in mind that the abolition of the compulsory retirement age is going to mean that more and more people will be working longer, so a more mature workforce is going to be the norm.

## I don't have any networking connections

Unless you stay in a sealed room for most of your day, you are bound to know people with whom you can network.

Your first port of call is family and friends. They are your warmest personal contacts, yet probably the most underused in networking terms. Whether you're a graduate or a more

> I happened to talk to a fellow dog walker and started talking about work. She told me her husband had just started work at the local factory and they were recruiting a lot of people. I sent my application in and that's how I got my job.  **Harriet**

mature job-seeker you should be asking all your family members and friends for any introductions and advice on getting your next job. You don't know who your family and friends know until you ask. (See Chapter 20 for more advice on how family and friends can help your career.) Beyond that, remember that anyone you meet in whatever circumstance could be a helpful contact. A client told me that he was catching a train recently and started talking to someone he recognised as one of the dads involved in running his son's football team. Their conversation turned to work and he offered to forward his CV to the relevant manager. The guy clearly put in a good word for him, he got a meeting and was subsequently hired.

---

**TIP** Exercise 42 (p215) will help you draw up your contact list.

---

Actively go out and network with people. Go to conferences, professional associations and community events to talk to people there.

Lastly, social media has developed all kinds of ways that people can come together to chat online. Join LinkedIn to build your online business profile and connect with those you know as well as new contacts through joining relevant interest groups. Facebook is a way of keeping in touch easily with family and friends and asking informally for advice and information.

> **TIP** If you are on Facebook, make sure that you keep your business and personal life separate.

## ✳ I'm worried that my career to date will be viewed negatively

It may be that you have had a number of shorter-term jobs, a career break, a period of unemployment, or that you left your last job in unhappy circumstances. Most people, if you ask them about their career, will have had some bumpier times.

There are two things to remember. First, downplay whatever the issue is rather than drawing attention to it. For instance, using a functional CV that lists all your relevant skills and experiences on the front page and relegates your employment dates to the second page can reduce the visibility of any career irregularities that would be very noticeable on a chronological CV.

Second, prospective employers will be largely influenced by how you talk about those problems, rather than the problem itself. Avoid the temptation to justify yourself by blaming others. Candidates who criticise past employers and blame them for their woes are very unattractive to an employer, no matter how true their claims are.

If you have been made redundant, as many people have at some point in their careers, talk about it as a tough business decision that the organisation made about your department, rather than a personal tragedy for you. If you didn't stay very long in one job, rather than talking negatively about how awful it was, find a positive rationale for leaving – such as a new opportunity that was simply too good to miss.

Most people's careers have ups and downs. Take it in your stride – focus on the positives and the employer is likely to view it positively too.

## ✳ *It's such a competitive job market – there's no way I'm going to stand out*

It is undeniably a tough job market right now and the job you want other people want too. It may therefore seem surprising that many employers, even now, complain that when it comes to candidates, they don't feel spoilt for choice. This is not due to a shortage of people able to do the job, but because most candidates do not market themselves as persuasively as they might. This includes submitting a CV with errors, interviewing badly, or failing to understand the employers' requirements. Chapter 21 gives you tips on how to perfect your sales pitch, to help you stand out from the crowd but, wherever you can, get some advice and feedback from career professionals or recruiters to maximise your chances of being shortlisted.

> **TIP** In a Personal Career Management survey, nine out of 10 CVs we had been sent from enquirers contained errors, poor content and presentation.

# 20 GETTING A HELPING HAND

I n Chapter 19 we looked at some of the common career blocks that surface when people are trying to progress their career. One of the most helpful resources for countering those blocks is the support of other people.

People often feel apprehensive about asking other people for advice. However, if you ask nicely, are duly appreciative and mindful of their time, then most people are very happy to help. In fact it's one of the things that people like doing best – telling others how they should be doing it.

In this chapter we look at who can help and how. You will also develop your own contact list of people whose input will be useful in the pursuit of your career goals (Exercise 42).

## *Professional career support*

You may benefit from working with a career management company to accelerate your career journey by using the additional career services they can provide. These can include career analysis, careers information, job market research services, help devising your self-marketing materials and practical job search support in the implementation of your career plan. If you have found it difficult to get high-quality, impartial feedback and advice, perhaps because you are working in a senior role, a professional career coach will be of benefit. Many people also benefit from the regular interaction of working with a coach and the practical and emotional support this provides during a period of transition.

> **TIP** If you are leaving your company because of redundancy or through a compromise agreement, then ask if they will help pay for career coaching or outplacement support to help you find your next job. There are tax and VAT advantages for you if it is included as part of an exit agreement.

The career coaching industry is unregulated in the UK, so choose a company that adheres to a recognised code of practice for the industry such as the CIPD's. Many companies offer a free initial meeting and this is an excellent opportunity for you to find out more about the company, its staff and its services. Reputable companies will always provide full written information about the services on offer, the resources available and the costs involved. There should never be any secrecy regarding this.

If you are looking for career coaching, check out the Personal Career Management site, www.personalcareermanagement.com, as this will give you a good indication of the kind of services on offer, the standards to expect and likely costs.

# *Family and friends*

Your family and friends will want to help you, but sometimes they are not sure how to. Always share with your loved ones exactly what you are looking for next career-wise. They are the warmest networking contacts you have, but probably the most underused.

> **TIP** Tell your family and friends what you are looking for. Don't assume they know.

I was recently talking to a graduate who wanted to work in the NHS but was finding it difficult to get anywhere. I asked her if she knew of anyone who worked in the NHS. 'Only my sister!' she said as though this didn't count. Following my advice, she asked her sister to put in a word with the HR department and she was offered some work experience which led to her subsequently being chosen for a graduate trainee role in the NHS.

Your loved ones may also be able to help with practical tasks such as checking your CV for errors or choosing an interview outfit. Career transition can be psychologically challenging, so be up-front with them about the emotional support and confidence-building you would find helpful.

If you have a partner, remember that they may be as worried as you about your career situation or indeed have their own career issues they are trying to resolve. The more mutually supportive you can be, the better equipped you will both be to handle any emotional ups and downs that arise.

## *Your manager*

Hopefully you have already been able to get feedback from your manager or an ex-manager using the 360-degree feedback exercise (Exercise 27, p123). If you haven't, you might find it easier to wait until you have a performance review or appraisal meeting with your manager or, if necessary, you could request a special meeting to discuss your career development.

Emphasise that you are interested in discussing your career because you want to improve your performance and progress in the future and that is why you would appreciate their advice and feedback.

> **TIP** If you show your employer that you are proactive about your career, they are more likely to see you as promotion material.

Share with them the kind of role that you would be interested in moving into in the future and any personal development goals. Ask for their advice on how you can get there. Go into the meeting with some suggestions of your own. For example, you could offer to:

- represent the department at external events
- spend some time with customers and suppliers
- write a research report
- work-shadow in another department.

If you can show that your career development will be good for the organisation, either because it will make you more effective in your current job or prepare you for promotion, your manager is more likely to be supportive.

> **TIP** If you are set on leaving the company, think carefully about how open you are about your intentions, as this may not be in your best interests while you remain in your role.

# *The HR department*

If your organisation has an HR team, ask for a meeting with them to find out more about career development opportunities within the organisation. Let them know what you are interested in and they may well have some relevant suggestions, including roles that may be on the horizon but not advertised yet. This will give you an opportunity to go and talk to the hiring manager ahead of time to declare your interest and suitability.

> **TIP** It's not the HR department's job to manage your career: it's yours! But they can be very helpful if you talk to them.

Even if there are no suitable vacancies, your HR department may be able to suggest career development opportunities which could take you closer to achieving your career goals. Many big organisations have a fast-track talent pool. If you're not sure, find out if they have one and what you need to do to be considered. Other development opportunities could include:

- internal and external training courses
- secondment
- volunteering on a project group
- having a mentor or mentoring others
- e-learning programmes
- organising a corporate event
- inducting new recruits and training others
- involvement in employer-sponsored volunteering.

If your organisation doesn't have an HR team, this discussion is more likely to take place with your manager or perhaps another senior manager whose responsibilities encompass HR.

> **TIP** Remember that whoever you are talking to about your career development, you should be asking for advice but also going in prepared with some ideas of your own. If your ideas are low-cost, easy to arrange and you offer to make up any time that is lost, it is much more likely that the employer will agree to them.

## Colleagues

If you work for a large organisation, try to build up a grapevine of contacts throughout the organisation. Go for lunch or a coffee with more distant colleagues to find out what is happening in their part of the organisation. It will give you a very different perspective and alert you to potential opportunities.

However, be a bit careful about how much you confide in colleagues, especially if your career goals are likely to impact on them or the organisation. Sometimes it is advisable to be discreet rather than too open.

## Customers and suppliers

In the course of your work you come into contact with many external people. Think about all the people you interact with every day. Many an employee has jumped ship to work with an organisation that was originally their customer. If you have a good working relationship with an external company, they may see you as potentially a good member of staff for them. This situation needs to be handled carefully as you don't want to compromise your relationship with either the customer or your own organisation.

When I lost my job I contacted the suppliers I had worked with. I had been a tough negotiator so I figured they would want me on their side next time. I was right! *Anita*

However, there is no harm in asking how they recruit their staff because you might be interested in applying to them in the future. If there is something suitable, they will probably tell you, but if not, you will have planted a seed that means that they may well come back to you at a later date.

> **TIP** If you do end up working for a company that has a relationship with your own, assure both companies that you will not be spilling any commercially sensitive information; stress that your aim is to use your knowledge of working on both sides to improve upon the relationship even further.

# *Professional forums*

Volunteer for opportunities where you can represent the company externally and which will bring you into contact with other people and their organisations. This could include helping out at exhibition stands, going to conferences, or reporting back from industry forums.

> I got my last job as a result of a casual conversation over coffee with someone who turned out to be the finance director of a competitor.
>
> **Henry**

One of the main purposes of these events is networking, sharing information, checking out the competition and discussing business challenges. Swap business cards where you can, follow up with an email – and use those connections when appropriate.

# *Mentors*

A mentor is normally someone in your field who has a more senior background than you, and who is happy to give you the benefit of their wisdom and experience. They can be especially useful if you are working towards a promotion or need a sounding board in a new job.

> A mentor is a more experienced individual willing to share knowledge with someone less experienced in a relationship of mutual trust
>
> **David Clutterbuck**

You may already have someone whom you have been using informally as a mentor. This might be an ex-manager, colleague or friend of the family whose advice you have always appreciated.

If you haven't anyone currently, it is worth considering who might be a good sounding board for you in respect of your career. It can be a very informal relationship with the odd lunch here and there; or you can, if they are happy to do so, arrange more regular meetings. However, as the relationship is generally an unpaid one, you will need to be mindful about how much time they may want to commit to mentoring you. If you want a more formal mentoring relationship it's recommended that you discuss expectations right from the outset.

> **TIP** Some large organisations, such as the civil service for example, may have a formal mentoring scheme in place.

Many professional associations provide mentoring schemes. For instance MentorSET is a UK-based initiative organised by the Women's Engineering Society and offers a mentoring scheme to help women working in the science, technology, engineering and mathematics industries. Mentoring schemes are often targeted at specific groups of people such as young people, newly qualified professionals in a particular field or certain ethnic groups. Look on the internet for mentoring schemes that may be appropriate for you.

### ✳ Tips on working with a mentor

- Find someone you feel you can learn from.
- Agree on what you both want and can give to the relationship.
- Be clear about boundaries – for example their availability, confidentiality, etc.

> **TIP** You should expect advice, not intervention, from your mentor. Your mentor will not 'fix' things on your behalf.

## Role model

In Part 2 we looked at the early influence of role models on your personal and career development. Role models can continue to be helpful for you. They may provide inspiration as well as very practical learning. For instance, if you are a female entrepreneur, follow the progress of women in your industry who have set up successful businesses. Read any articles or books they have written. Attend any speaker events where they will be appearing and go and talk to them afterwards. It's always useful to learn from

> Where you are right now doesn't have to determine where you'll end up. You write your own destiny. You make your own future.
> **Barack Obama**

other people who have faced similar challenges to you and emerged the other side.

Now you've considered who may be able to help you, let's draw up your own contact list.

# *Exercise 42: Your contact list*

1. Write down below a list of people you feel can help you with advice, feedback or potential job contacts. If there are certain individuals you really don't want to approach even if they may have great contacts, perhaps because you have had a difficult relationship in the past, don't bother. However, if you've had a good relationship – what are you waiting for?

2. Highlight those who are most likely to be helpful and arrange to talk to them first.

*(Continued)*

⭐ **Example**

Pete, HR at his company, dad's company, all the suppliers I worked with, ex-boss, old colleagues at Zenith Enterprises, course tutor, people at church, recruiter who placed me in the job, sister-in-law …

*Greg*

# 21 THE ART OF SELF-PROMOTION

Whatever your career aspirations or objectives, you are going to need to learn how to talk positively about yourself to others. You must be able to impress people in your current organisation as well as prospective employers, recruiters and networking contacts.

This is trickier than it looks. From childhood we are brought up to believe that anything that borders on self-promotion is 'big-headed' and socially unacceptable. We are unused to talking positively about ourselves to others and many people experience a real sense of discomfort when they have to 'sell' themselves to a potential employer.

However, the art of 'self-promotion' is one that you need to acquire in order to get on in your career. When you are looking for a new job, you will be asked detailed and fairly intrusive questions about all aspects of your skills, abilities and personality by complete strangers. They will judge you based on the content of what you say and how you say it. You may be applying for the perfect job for you, but your success will hinge on your ability to sell yourself effectively.

This chapter looks at the key ingredients you need to have in place as part of your personal sales and marketing campaign.

## *Your CV*

You should always have an up-to-date CV that positions you as the perfect candidate for your next role, rather than simply recording what you have done in the past. Here are some key tips.

## ✳ Research

Find out as much as you can about the job you want and the employer's requirements. Study advertisements and job descriptions, talk to recruiters or those who work in a similar role and ask their advice on what gives a candidate a competitive edge. (See Chapter 17 to remind yourself about this.)

## ✳ Match

Use the information gained from your research to help you show in your CV that you have the specific skills, experience and approach required. Ensure these key aspects are included within the first half page of your CV so the recruiter can quickly see your suitability. See Exercise 33 on interpreting job advertisements.

## ✳ Evidence

Unsubstantiated claims won't work. You need to prove you have what they need. So instead of saying on your CV that you have 'good communication skills', give an example of where you demonstrated this to good effect, for example 'Invited to join the sales bid team because of my ability to translate technical detail into language that the customer could understand.' See Exercise 13 on assessing your skills.

## ✳ Language

Avoid long sentences and using 'I' ('I did this…', 'I did that…'). Instead use bullet points, e.g. 'Led this…', Created that…', which will seem much more dynamic. Never include any criticisms of others, business setbacks or failures unless you were able to turn them around.

## ✳ Professional presentation

This needs to be of the highest standard with a layout that is consistent, attractive and easy to read. All spelling and grammar needs to be checked and double-checked.

## ✳ Format

Avoid complex formatting, such as columns, tables and graphics, on your CV: this can interfere with the way your CV is stored on the recruitment database.

> **TIP** My book, *You're Hired! How to Write a Brilliant CV* (Trotman, 2009), gives you more detailed information and templates you can use for your CV.

## ⊁ Audience

Tailor each CV to its audience, highlighting the things that you know will be of most interest to them. This may mean that you have a few different CVs, each tweaked to the requirements of each individual job and employer.

> **TIP** Refer back to Part 4 where we looked at your career capital to draw on the aspects which are most relevant to the job for which you are applying.

# Covering letters and emails

Do not underestimate the importance of the covering letter or email that accompanies your CV. It can positively influence or scupper your chances of success.

- Always write a covering letter or email rather than sending an unaccompanied CV.
- Ensure you spell correctly the name of the person it is addressed to. Nothing irritates people more than their name being misspelled.
- Write the letter from the standpoint of demonstrating the advantages to the employer of meeting with you. Tell them how can you help them and their organisation by increasing their profit, efficiency, solving a problem or meeting a challenge they have.
- Make sure the spelling and presentation is 100% accurate and looks professional. Avoid text speak on emails – it is not considered acceptable in this context.

# Online marketing campaign

Even if you are looking for a role as an employee, you should conduct a marketing and PR campaign similar to that you would use if you were running your own business. If you are looking to position yourself as an expert in your field, or simply increase your visibility in a particular area, writing articles, blogging, tweeting and joining online discussions are a great way to generate interest and get yourself known. Increase your personal PR by writing regularly about relevant topics to strengthen your online presence, impress potential employers and help you connect with others interested in the same topics.

> **TIP** You can find advice on using social media like LinkedIn and Twitter for your career on www.personalcareermanagement.com

## ⋇ LinkedIn

If you have not already done so, create a profile on www.linkedin.com so that you can advertise your skills, abilities and experience to recruiters and prospective employers who frequently trawl through the site for candidates. LinkedIn is the equivalent of a card in the newsagent's window of the professional business community. Recruiters will visit the site looking for suitable candidates, so make sure that you are visible.

> **TIP** If you are a business professional and you are not listed on LinkedIn, people will assume you are technologically out of date, are poorly connected or have something to hide.

On your profile, make sure that you:

- check that the information is consistent with your CV – otherwise it will raise queries about the accuracy of the information you have supplied
- supply a professional-looking photograph rather than a fun one
- ask people you have worked with to write you an endorsement and post it on your profile. You can also upload presentations and videos
- treat your LinkedIn updates like personal press releases, but keep them business-focused
- join online networking groups to boost your visibility by participating in online discussions.

> **TIP** Ensure that any online presence you have is business appropriate. Employers may Google you, so make sure that all online information about you presents you in an attractive and positive light.

## ☀ Twitter

Create a Twitter account at www.twitter.com as another way of raising your visibility in your field, helping you connect with others and hear about online jobs.

- Make sure that you tweet about business and professional successes, interesting activities you are involved in and events you have attended.
- Your tweets should always show you in a positive, business-like manner.
- Avoid trivia or anything that you wouldn't want a prospective employer to know about you.
- Use Twitter to follow people you are interested in and also access jobs posted on Twitter.

You can follow Personal Career Management on twitter at @changecareer, or me on @corinnemills to receive regular career tips and information.

## ☀ Website

If you are a creative professional such as a writer, artist, web designer or cake maker, you should have a website where you can include examples of your work for prospective employers or customers to see. Your website should include:

- details of your skills and experience
- projects worked on
- achievements
- examples of your work in photos, pdfs or hyperlinks
- testimonials from customers
- contact information.

> **TIP** You can get free online listings for your business through Google and other online directories.

# Your elevator pitch

If you meet someone for the first time, particularly if it is in a professional setting, they are likely to ask you what you do. This is your opportunity to clearly convey not only what you do but also what you *want* to be doing.

Sometimes this is called your 'elevator pitch', the idea being that in the 30–60 seconds it takes to get in the lift with someone and arrive at your chosen floor you have succinctly conveyed the key messages you want people to understand about you. It is usually the opener to a longer conversation where you find out more about the other party, establish any joint interests or connections and how you may be able to help each other.

The key components of your elevator pitch are:

- the skills and experience you want to be known for
- relevant employers worked with or projects worked on
- what you are looking for next, if appropriate
- asking the other person about themselves.

Your pitch should be delivered in a confident, clear manner. Practising this in advance is very helpful. Testing it out with people will help you to refine it. The more you practise it the more comfortable and relaxed you will become about delivering it.

## ⚹ Why is it important?

Most people, when asked to introduce themselves, do so apologetically as though they are embarrassed to talk about themselves. They downplay what they do, dismiss it as though it is not important and frequently use it to whinge about their job. This is an opportunity for you to connect with someone who could be your next employer or customer. If you give them relevant information and are positive and confident, the chances of them wanting to engage with you further are increased. Many coaching clients ask for help on this. It is one of the most important elements of your career management strategy – being able to talk about yourself positively to others.

> **TIP** Remember that any conversation needs to be two-way: if you show genuine interest in what the other person does, their concerns, challenges or successes, they are much more likely to return the favour.

# Interviews

This is the ultimate sales pitch scenario. You've got past the first hurdle: they obviously like your CV and have offered you an interview. Now you are the candidate trying to sell yourself to the employer for the vacancy.

## ✳ Interview preparation

Careful research and preparation are needed before you even get in the interview room if you are to stand the best chance of success. Your research should include:

- all the job details and selection criteria
- company facts such as size, turnover, market share, key products, sites, recent press releases
- looking at their closest competitors and how they compare
- understanding key challenges and trends for the company and their industry
- informal research – by talking to people who know the company.

This research will help you talk more knowledgably about why you think you are a good fit for the company. It will also demonstrate your keen interest and enthusiasm for the job as well as showing your professionalism and diligence. Work out what you think their priorities are in hiring a candidate and then consider how you can demonstrate that you meet all of these requirements.

Where you think the employer may be looking for something that you don't have, don't ignore it and hope for the best. Be proactive and think about how you might deal with this head on. This might involve:

- reading up on the area in question
- investigating courses that could help you bridge the gap quickly
- arranging relevant work experience
- identifying transferable or complementary skills: for example, while you may not be familiar with a particular database, you may have used similar ones in the past.

> **TIP** You're Hired! Interview: Tips and Techniques for a Brilliant Interview (Trotman, 2009) and You're Hired! Interview Answers: Impressive Answers to Tough Questions (Trotman, 2010) take you through each stage of the interview process in greater detail. If you are asked to do psychometric tests, have a look at You're Hired! Psychometric Tests: Proven Tactics to Help You Pass (Trotman, 2010).

At the interview, use real-life examples to illustrate your relevant skills and experience in action. Remember that, whatever the role, employers are always most interested in hearing about how you have added value to a company. Go back to Chapter 9 and the exercises you completed to remind yourself of some examples from your career.

> **TIP** If there is an opportunity to have an informal discussion with the relevant manager before the interview, always take advantage of this. You can then find out more about how the manager sees the role. Sometimes you will find that this has changed since the job description was written. It also gives you an early opportunity to sell yourself as the ideal candidate.

In your answers, be careful not to get bogged down in providing too much detail. Rehearse your answers to expected questions out loud and pare them down to the minimum, usually two or three sentences. The interviewer(s) will ask for more information if they need it.

## ⭑ Looking the part

Rightly or wrongly, your image will be a key factor in people's perception of you when going for a new job, or even at your current one. This is not about beauty: it is whether your personal appearance is in line with their expectations of what a successful candidate will look like.

Your choice of clothes can be a very powerful tool in persuading others of your workplace capabilities, and if you want to be taken seriously either by your existing or a new organisation, you will generally find it easier to progress your career if you comply with the organisation's dress code. In a very traditional organisation that may be a smart, pin-striped suit. In a creative industry it may be 'fashionably on-trend'. If you can get the dress code right, these are easy points in your favour.

> **TIP** If you are looking for promotion, dress as though you are already at that more senior level. It can help positively influence the perceptions of those around you.

# Your Career Action Plan

## PART 7

We've been on a long journey of self-discovery throughout this book and it is now time to start translating your research and the decisions you have made into action. We will chart exactly what you need to do to move on in your career and reach your goals. Throughout the book we have been collecting information that will feed into your Career Action Plan, which we will put together in Chapter 22.

We will also put together a Career Summary, using the exercises you have completed. This will be a document which will provide an easy reference for you about the important elements that have emerged from your career coaching experience.

## In this section we will:

✓ create your Career Action Plan

✓ look back on your career coaching journey, and summarise what you have learned.

# 22 CAREER ACTION PLAN

Y ou may know exactly what you need to do to progress your career, and in fact have already taken the first steps. If so, fantastic!

However, your career is not something that you fix overnight or even in a couple of weeks. It can be very easy to become distracted, let other things take priority, or become derailed if things don't happen as quickly as you had hoped.

This is where a written action plan can really help. First, writing down your goals makes them tangible and clear, rather than remaining as a vaguely expressed notion at the back of your head.

Second, your Career Action Plan will guide you as to what to do and when, outlining the steps you need to take in order to achieve your goals. You can then plan this into your diary rather than relying on spontaneous bursts of action as and when you remember.

Your Career Action Plan will be constantly evolving and need to be regularly reviewed but at least if you have a plan, you know where you are heading and how to get there.

Your action plan is made up of:

- Exercise 43: Your career goals – your long-term objective, and intermediate goals
- Exercise 44: Your career action task list, made up of SMART objectives
- Exercise 45: Your career action schedule – with target dates.

Once this is in place, we will look back on your career coaching journey in Chapter 23 and compile your Career Summary.

## Exercise 43: Your career goals

We are going to start your Career Action Plan using a mind-map exercise as in the following example. The aim here is to generate lots of ideas which we can use to write a more formal action plan.

### ✳ Example

In the example opposite, the central circle is the overall career objective related to your career decision in Exercise 39 (p186). The smaller circles represent the intermediate career goals relevant to the overall goal. Each of the smaller circles then branches into the tasks that need to be undertaken to achieve each specific career goal.

Let's use this model to start thinking about your career campaign.

1.  In the central circle on p230, write the overall career objective you pinpointed in Exercise 39 (p186). This may be an immediate need or a longer-term aspiration, and it should be as clear and direct as possible. You may also want to review Exercise 3 (Work/life balance assessment, p21), Exercise 6 (I want ..., p35) and Exercise 30 (Visualising the future, p135).

2.  Identify the smaller career goals that will help you achieve your overall career objective. Examples might include:
    - personal development goals – such as acquiring the technical knowledge you need
    - bridging skill or experience gaps – such as taking on voluntary work for those returning to work after a break
    - making changes in your current role – such as improving your job satisfaction
    - tackling the external job market – such as getting shortlisted for the jobs you want
    - personal goals – such as work/life balance.

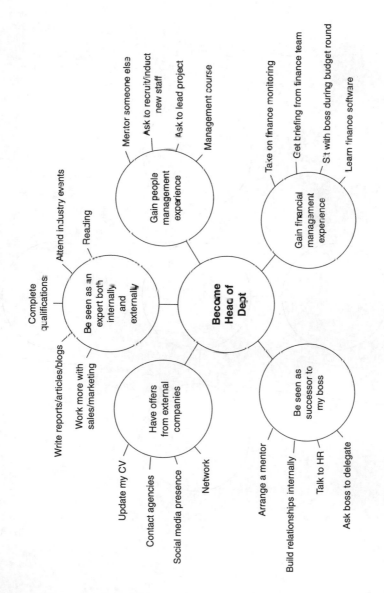

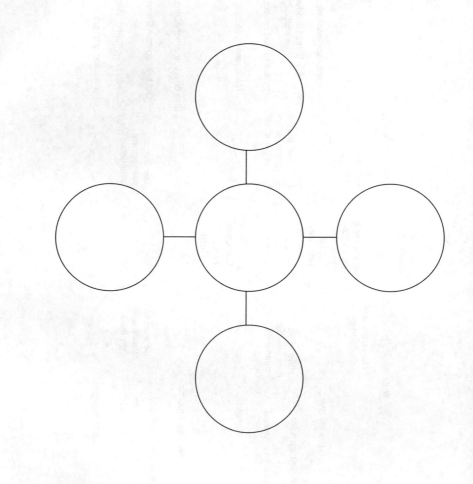

3. Add as many of your career goals as you can to the diagram, aiming for a minimum of four. You may want to look back to the Actions section in your Reflections exercises at the end of each part of the book to ensure you don't miss anything.

4. Once you have entered your career goals, write down all the practical tasks you need to undertake to help you achieve those goals. Add as many suggestions as you can to the above diagram, with each task branching off from the relevant goal. You should have a minimum of five tasks per goal, but add as many as you can. You can always edit them down later.

> **TIP** Transfer your mind-map onto a separate piece of paper if you need more room.

Below are some ideas for tasks as a prompt to help you.

> **TIP** Look back at your action points in your Reflections Exercises to remind you of what you can do that will make a difference.

## ✳ Ideas for your Career Action Plan

| Getting organised | Relevant? |
|---|:---:|
| Get the computer equipment, software, internet access I need | ☐ |
| Ensure my mobile voicemail works and message is appropriate | ☐ |
| Allocate a set time/day I will work on my career goals/plan | ☐ |
| Create document to track job applications or conversations with recruiters | ☐ |
| Use an electronic or paper calendar to remind me of my career tasks | ☐ |
| **Preparing for the job market** | |
| Devise CV(s) using relevant help | ☐ |

*(Continued)*

| | |
|---|---|
| Get independent feedback to make sure CV is effective | ☐ |
| Read about different job search strategies, e.g. adverts, agencies, direct approaches | ☐ |
| Develop my 'elevator pitch' to introduce myself to strangers | ☐ |
| Practise my interview skills and get some feedback | ☐ |
| Rehearse telephone calls to recruiters | ☐ |
| Buy an interview outfit, get a haircut, update my look | ☐ |
| Organise business cards | ☐ |
| Contact recruitment agencies and headhunters and post my CV(s) on line | ☐ |
| Apply for a target number of jobs each week/month | ☐ |
| Proactively contact a target number of companies each week/month | ☐ |
| Arrange a target number of networking meetings each week/month | ☐ |
| Read local paper/journals to identify companies that may need my skills | ☐ |
| Use my grapevine to keep eyes and ears open | ☐ |
| **Using social media** | |
| Join LinkedIn (see p220 for more on what you should do) | ☐ |
| Ensure privacy settings are set on Facebook account | ☐ |
| Link with interesting companies and participate in their online communities | ☐ |
| Use Twitter to help my job search (see p221) | ☐ |
| Seek out other online professional forums for interacting with fellow professionals, information sharing | ☐ |

*(Continued)*

| | |
|---|---|
| Follow @changecareer and @corinnemills on Twitter for career tips and advice | ☐ |

**Increase visibility in my field**

| | |
|---|---|
| Write articles, media commentary or blogs on my subject or specialist area | ☐ |
| Train others, become a lecturer, speak at conferences | ☐ |
| Set up a website to display examples of my work | ☐ |
| Join relevant professional associations or forums and attend events | ☐ |
| Volunteer for a committee role | ☐ |

**Career development with my current employer**

| | |
|---|---|
| Talk to: my manager, HR and decision-makers within the organisation | ☐ |
| Ask for feedback | ☐ |
| Join a cross-organisational project group | ☐ |
| Volunteer to write a report | ☐ |
| Organise a charity event | ☐ |
| Arrange a mentor | ☐ |
| Ask to attend conferences | ☐ |
| Apply for internal vacancies | ☐ |
| Join cross-organisational working groups | ☐ |
| Meet for lunch with other colleagues | ☐ |
| Ask for additional responsibilities | ☐ |
| Ask for flexible working or reduced hours | ☐ |
| Arrange work experience in another department | ☐ |

*(Continued)*

| | |
|---|---|
| Ask for a secondment or a sabbatical | ☐ |
| Ask for a pay rise | ☐ |

**Personal and professional development**

| | |
|---|---|
| Keep up-to-date with developments in my field, e.g. new software or legal changes | ☐ |
| Investigate training courses, conferences, workshops | ☐ |
| Study for a qualification | ☐ |
| Create a written learning log to capture and reflect on key learning challenges | ☐ |
| Join or create a group of fellow learners eg an action learning set or peer supervision group | ☐ |
| Read relevant books and journals | ☐ |
| Work with a career coach | ☐ |
| Upgrade my professional memberships | ☐ |
| Undertake voluntary work to extend my skills and experience | ☐ |

**Self-employment**

| | |
|---|---|
| Research different self-employment options | ☐ |
| Investigate franchises | ☐ |
| Conduct customer and market research | ☐ |
| Create a business plan | ☐ |
| Review finances and investment | ☐ |
| Develop marketing materials | ☐ |
| Talk to an accountant and the bank | ☐ |

*(Continued)*

| **Personal** | |
|---|---|
| Talk to my partner about my career goals and how they can help | ☐ |
| Enlist support of family and friends | ☐ |
| Ensure quality personal time for self and family | ☐ |
| Get healthy by taking exercise and watching diet | ☐ |
| Build confidence through self help books, counselling or courses | ☐ |
| Improve social life | ☐ |

Your mind-map should now be bursting with ideas about practical things you can do to achieve your career goals.

# Be SMART

The next stage of your Career Action Plan is to organise these ideas into a schedule.

You may have heard of the SMART rules for goal-setting and how helpful they can be when devising personal and business-related goals. The SMART rules remind us that if our goal-setting it is to be workable, it must be:

- **S**pecific: It is important to be detailed and precise. If there is any vagueness, this is an indicator of a stumbling block ahead and it needs addressing.
- **M**easurable: Identify success criteria so that you can determine whether or not you have been successful. For instance, instead of saying you will network, set yourself a target of how many networking meetings you will have in a month.
- **A**chievable: Ensure you are realistic. Make sure your goals are stretching but doable. Ambitious goals should be broken into smaller, more achievable steps.
- **R**elevant: Everything in your Career Action Plan should be relevant to your overall career objectives. Keep it focused.
- **T**ime-bound: Set target dates and deadlines for the goals and tasks to keep momentum and avoid procrastination.

Using the SMART criteria and your answers to Exercise 43, we are now going to write down a task list.

## Exercise 44: Your career action task list

**44**

1. Write down each of your career goals and how you will know when you have achieved it, for example by completing a qualification or being invited to an interview.

2. Itemise the relevant tasks you will undertake for each career goal, giving yourself a target date for completion.

3. For ongoing tasks like reading a professional journal, the target should indicate how many times you will do that task per week or month.

Two examples are outlined below.

### ✳ Example

---

## CAREER GOAL 1

**For my expertise to be sought out both internally and externally.**

I will know I am successful when the management team start asking me directly for advice and I am asked to give presentations internally and externally at industry events, on project groups and at sales meetings.

### Tasks/activities

- Ask immediately if I can accompany the sales team as the in-house technical expert.
- Complete my postgraduate qualification in 2013.
- Attend conferences and speaker events at least three times a year and get to know the organising committee(s).
- Read my industry journal every month and subscribe to newsletters on industry topics.
- Become a volunteer committee member for my professional association at AGM in April.

---

*(Continued)*

- Offer to write a report on industry trends and distribute it to the managers by June.
- Find a project group that I can get involved with by March.
- Represent my boss at least once in the next year at one of the cross-industry functions.

## CAREER GOAL 2

**When my boss retires, for me to be considered as the natural successor.**

I want to be offered his job when he leaves next year.

### Tasks/activities

- Ask my manager at appraisal meeting in March if they can delegate more tasks/responsibilities to help my development.
- Make sure that from now on when I do reports for senior management team they are aware that I have produced them.
- Develop strong working relationships with other departments in coming year so that I become their main liaison person. Aim to visit all six departments by end of year
- Arrange an external mentor for advice about making the move to more senior level by end of year.
- Talk to HR before February so that they know my career objectives.
- Talk to my boss's boss in the coming year.

*Manjit*

Now it's your turn!

## ✳ *My career goals*

### CAREER GOAL 1
Tasks/activities

### CAREER GOAL 2
Tasks/activities

## CAREER GOAL 3
Tasks/activities

## CAREER GOAL 4
Tasks/activities

Now that you have a clear list of what you are going to do to achieve each goal, let's organise your tasks in date order so that you can integrate these activities into your diary. This is a good opportunity for you to double-check that you are being realistic in terms of your time schedule.

> **TIP** Things can often take longer than you think, so be generous with the amount of time you allocate: but once you have finalised your schedule, always do your best to keep to it.

## Exercise 45: Your career action schedule

1. Add real dates to the schedule below so you know the actual calendar date for the completion of each task.

2. Review your task list and group the tasks in date order so that you can see clearly on a calendar what you are going to do when.

3. Complete the following schedule.

An example is given on pp242–243.

What will I do tomorrow?

What will I do by the end of next week?

*(Continued)*

What will I do by the end of the month?

What will I do by the end of 3 months?

What will I do in 6 months?

Within a year, I will...

What will I have done within 3–5 years?

## ⚝ *Example*

Tomorrow (__/__/__) I will...

- see if there is any help available for women returners at my local job centre.

By the end of next week (__/__/__) I will...

- find out about local colleges providing IT skills courses
- organise a personal email address
- change my voicemail message so it doesn't have the kids on it.

By the end of the month (__/__/__) I will...

- speak to the office at the school to find out about any job vacancies there
- offer to help brother-in-law with some of his admin to get experience
- investigate after-school childcare and costs
- talk to my friend Carol who runs a recruitment agency.

By the end of 3 months (__/__/__) I will...

- start doing some voluntary work so I have experience to put on my CV
- contact my old boss and some of my work colleagues
- have developed a CV that I can send out for jobs
- be looking at the local paper for jobs.

Within 6 months, 30/6/12 (__/__/__) I will...

- be applying for jobs with my new CV – at least one a week
- develop a covering letter I can adapt for different jobs
- learn how to apply for jobs online
- learn how to do a LinkedIn profile
- do some interview skills training to build confidence.

Within a year (__/__/__) I will...

- be working in a part-time job or in a voluntary role which will help me get one
- have all my IT skills up to date
- feel much more confident about going back to work because I have gained some practical work experience
- investigate teacher training courses and also other career options for potential retraining.

*(Continued)*

Within 3–5 years (__/__/__) I will have...

- maybe done a teacher training course or other course
- investigated possibilities for setting up my own business from home.

*Jo*

Well done! You have now created your Career Action Plan, so you know exactly what you need to do and when. Whether you use a paper diary or a calendar that is integrated with your computer software or phone, make sure you schedule in the above activities.

I found writing my Career Action Plan quite challenging. However, it was because I had planned in the routine stuff, targeting myself for four good networking meetings a month, that I heard about the job from Ian. I might not have spoken to him otherwise. *Rob*

**TIP** Make sure your plan is highly visible and accessible, and provides you with regular reminders about your goals and target dates.

# Progress review

You may find that your career goals and objectives start to change as you progress through the year. There may be changes of plan: for instance, you might have secured your new job more quickly than you thought; or the threat of redundancy may give you a new sense of urgency.

If this is the case, just amend your plan accordingly, but don't, whatever you do, let it lapse. Review your plan after six months to check progress and include any new career priorities.

It is also recommended that you complete all three career action planning exercises afresh each year. Make a note of the progress you made during the past year, and then reappraise your career goals and the career activities needed for the year ahead. Some elements may remain the same, but you may be quite surprised at how much has changed, especially if you have been making good progress with your plan.

# *Rewards and celebrations*

Whether you have achieved one of your main career goals or simply plucked up the courage to do something positive which took you out of your comfort zone, you should reward yourself.

If it is a major achievement, such as the new job you wanted – celebrate. Go out for dinner, have a party, go to the pub! Announce the news on your LinkedIn and Twitter profiles. Notify the trade press if appropriate, especially if you want to grab the attention of recruiters or potential employers for the future.

You should also reward yourself for anything you have achieved that was personally very challenging. For instance, if you are a nervous networker, but successfully spoke to two complete strangers at an event, this is worthy of a well-deserved pat on the back. Tell others what you have done and they may well give you a pat too!

Don't beat yourself up, as some people do, for feeling stupid that it felt difficult at all. Overcoming personal obstacles, whatever they might be, are evidence that you are growing in your capabilities and confidence. This is hugely significant and the more positive reinforcement and encouragement you receive, the more likely that what once felt a huge deal becomes a regular habit.

Well done! You now have a Career Action Plan to help you move your career forward in your chosen direction.

# 23 YOUR CAREER SUMMARY

Y our Career Action Plan is now in place to help you focus your energies on achieving your career goals.

The career coaching process has offered a very in-depth analysis of your career and the way ahead. Throughout the book we have included reflections exercises for you to capture any thoughts, ideas and emotions that were prompted during the individual sections. In this chapter we bring together your key insights and findings from the whole book to help you summarise your career coaching experience.

I have also included space in this chapter for you to send a direct message to yourself so that you can capture how you are feeling about your career at this point.

## Exercise 46: My career document

### ☆ My career goals

List your career goals – you will have fine-tuned these in your Career Action Plan in Exercise 43 (p228), but remind yourself of your answers in Exercise 6 (p35) as well.

**46**

*(Continued)*

## ⚡ *My career capital*

1. Review Exercises 13–22 to record here the main elements of your career capital and what you have to offer a prospective employer. These could include the following.
   - Your key skills (Exercise 13, p78)
   - Your achievements (Exercise 14, p85)
   - The value you add to a company (Exercise 15, p91)
   - Your professional credibility (Exercise 16, p94)
   - The training you have undertaken (Exercise 17, p96)
   - The knowledge you possess (Exercise 18, p98)
   - Any additional work experience or voluntary work (Exercise 19, p101)
   - Relevant interests and information (Exercises 20 and 22, p102, p104)
   - Your network, if impressive (Exercise 21, p103).

2. Note the key points of what makes up your career capital below.

*(Continued)*

## ✳ *My personal strengths*

1. Identify from your career history examples of positive behaviours such as resilience, hard work, relationship building (Exercise 11, p65).
2. Look at Exercises 24–26 (pp113–121), which examined your workstyle. Pick out your positive traits and the organisational contexts which would best suit you.
3. Review the positive feedback you received from others in Exercise 27 (p123).

### ✳ Blocks and bridges

1. Review Exercise 41 on p194 where we looked at career blocks that could be holding you back.
2. What are the things that might get in the way of your career progress?
3. How will you overcome them? Look back at the advice in Chapter 19 to help you.

| What might get in the way | What will help |
| --- | --- |
| | |

# *Exercise 47: Message to myself*

## 47

Imagine yourself in a year's time. If you could talk to yourself from the future and give your present-day self some advice, what would you say? What positive words of advice and encouragement can you offer? What pep talk can you give?

Make this message to yourself as heartfelt as you can. You could include any of the following.

> It is not the mountain we conquer but ourselves.                    *Edmund Hillary*

- Why your career goals are important to you.
- What difference would achieving your goals make to you or others?
- Advice on how to overcome any anticipated obstacles.
- Words of encouragement and confidence-building.
- Addressing any fears or concerns.
- Reminding yourself of the support you have around you.
- Focus on your capabilities and strengths.

## Exercise 48: Final reflections

Reviewing your career coaching journey throughout this book, make a note of your reflections and any thoughts or ideas that have surfaced. Use your reflections exercises at the end of each section to help you bring together what you have learned. This might include the answers to these questions.

- What have you learned?
- What, if anything, has changed?
- What might you do differently in the future?
- Where is there work still to be done?
- Any other comments.

> **TIP** See Exercises 7 (p37), 12 (p71), 23 (p105), 28 (p128) and 40 (p188) for your past reflections exercises.

*(Continued)*

# AND FINALLY...

We've travelled a long way in the course of this book, from your earliest memories to your future career vision. We have explored, deconstructed and market-tested every inch of your career to ensure that you understand it from an objective perspective. We have looked at your options, made considered and well-researched decisions and, in the last part of this book, we created a plan to turn your career aspirations into reality.

I hope that you have found this book insightful, thought-provoking and of practical use. Its key message is that if you want to have a rewarding career, it takes more than just working hard in the job. You have to **manage** your career and that takes thoughtfulness, research, planning, asking for the help of others and lots of action!

I hope that this book has also opened up some new career possibilities for you to consider. Whatever

> Some people dream of success while others wake up and work hard at it   *Anon*

your circumstances, there are always options, whether you want to stay within your current organisation, move to a new company, change career direction or start your own business. Your career development is in your own hands.

This is not to say that it is always easy to make the changes you want. Sometimes it isn't. But if you remain focused, follow your plan, see any setbacks as an opportunity to learn, and keep the energy consistently high, you will achieve your goals.

We may be coming to the end of this book and the career coaching process, but your career will be a continuing story rather than a closed chapter. I hope that this book has laid the foundations for an exciting new career adventure. It is over to you from here!

I wish you every success.

*Corinne Mills*

If you would like to share your story of how this book has helped you, we would love to hear from you.

Email us at mystory@personalcareermanagment.com

# USEFUL RESOURCES

## *Career coaching*

If you have enjoyed working through this book, you may be interested in some real-life career coaching.

Personal Career Management, which was founded by Corinne Mills, offers one-to-one specialist career coaching and outplacement services. Their team of coaches help with career analysis and planning as well as providing advice and support on all aspects of job hunting including CVs, interviews, networking and using social media. They also provide market intelligence and research services.

Their coaching clients are drawn from a wide range of occupations and industry sectors, both from the UK and abroad. Many of them are seeking to explore their career options, change sector or role, or improve their job hunting success. Personal Career Management also work with corporate clients ranging from FTSE 100 companies to charities, public sector organisations and SMEs.

The company are career experts for the *Guardian*, Telegraph Jobs, Monster and for several professional institutes. They also frequently appear on television, on radio and in the national and trade press advising on career related issues.

You can find out more about their services via the Personal Career Management website which also contains many useful free career resources including articles, career tips and videos on career-related topics.

| | |
|---|---|
| Website | www.personalcareermanagement.com |
| Email | Info@personalcareermanagement.com |
| Telephone | +44 (0) 845 686 0745 |
| Facebook | www.facebook.com/careermanagement |
| Twitter | @changecareer |

You can find downloads for selected exercises from this book at www.personalcareermanagement.com/careercoach

# Recommended books

*You're Hired! How to Write a Brilliant CV* (Trotman, 2009)

*You're Hired! Interview: Tips and Techniques for a Brilliant Interview* (Trotman, 2009)

*You're Hired! Interview Answers: Impressive Answers to Tough Questions* (Trotman, 2010)

*You're Hired! Psychometric Tests: Proven Tactics to Help You Pass* (Trotman, 2010)

*You're Hired! CVs, Interviews and Psychometric Tests* (Trotman, 2011)

*Shine: Be an excellent employee, take control of your career and fulfil your potential* (Trotman, 2010)

*Start Your Own Business* 2011 and 2012 (Crimson Publishing, 2010 and 2011)

# Websites

## ⋇ Sector Skills Councils

These are correct at the time of going to press but are currently under government review.

| Sector Skills Council | Sector coverage |
|---|---|
| *Cogent* www.cogent-ssc.com | Bioscience, chemical, nuclear, oil and gas, petroleum and polymer industries |

*(Continued)*

| | |
|---|---|
| *Construction skills*<br>www.cskills.org | Construction |
| *Creative and cultural skills*<br>www.ccskills.org.uk | Craft, cultural heritage, design, literature, music, visual and performing arts |
| *e-skills*<br>www.e-skills.com | Information technology and telecommunications |
| *Energy and utilities skills*<br>www.euskills.co.uk | Electricity, gas, waste management and water industries |
| *Financial Skills Partnership*<br>www.financialskillspartnership.org.uk | Financial services, finance and accounting sectors |
| *GoSkills*<br>www.goskills.org | Passenger transport |
| *Improve*<br>www.improveltd.co.uk | Food and drink manufacturing and processing |
| *Institute of the Motor Industry*<br>www.motor.org.uk | The retail motor industry |
| *Lantra*<br>www.lantra.co.uk | Environmental and land-based industries |
| *People 1st*<br>www.people1st.co.uk | Hospitality, leisure, travel and tourism |
| *Proskills UK*<br>www.proskills.co.uk | Process and manufacturing industry |
| *SEMTA*<br>www.semta.org.uk | Science, engineering and manufacturing technologies (including composites) |
| *Skills for Care and Development*<br>www.skillsforcareanddevelopment.org.uk | Early years, children and young people's services; social work and social care for adults and children |
| *Skills for Health*<br>www.skillsforhealth.org.uk | The health sector across the UK |

*(Continued)*

| | |
|---|---|
| *Skills for Justice*<br>www.skillsforjustice.com | Community safety; courts, tribunals and prosecution; law enforcement; policing; legal services, etc. |
| *Skills for Logistics*<br>www.skillsforlogistics.org | Freight logistics industry and wholesale |
| *SkillsActive*<br>www.skillsactive.com | Active leisure, learning and well-being |
| *Skillset*<br>www.skillset.org | Broadcast, film, video, interactive media, publishing, advertising, fashion |
| *Skillsmart Retail*<br>www.skillsmartretail.com | Retail |
| *SummitSkills*<br>www.summitskills.org.uk | Building services, engineering |

## ✷ Job sites

| | |
|---|---|
| Monster | www.monster.co.uk |
| *Telegraph* | http://jobs.telegraph.co.uk |
| *Guardian* | http://jobs.guardian.co.uk |
| Reed | www.reed.co.uk |
| The Sun | www.jobs.thesun.co.uk |
| Jobsite | www.jobsite.co.uk |
| Total Jobs | www.totaljobs.com |
| CV Library | www.cv-library.co.uk |
| Fish 4 Jobs | www.fish4.co.uk |
| Job Search | www.jobsearch.co.uk |
| Job Serve | www.jobserve.com |

## ✷ Salary surveys

| | |
|---|---|
| Monster | www.monster.co.uk |
| Reed | www.reed.co.uk |
| My Salary | www.mysalary.co.uk |
| Michael Page | www.michaelpage.co.uk |
| Total Jobs | www.totaljobs.com |
| Pay Scale | www.payscale.com |
| Pay Wizard | www.paywizard.co.uk |

## ✴ Job-related websites for the over-50s

| | |
|---|---|
| Skilled People | www.skilledpeople.com |
| Prime 50 Plus | www.prime50plus.co.uk |
| Over Fifties Friends | www.overfiftiesfriends.co.uk |
| Later Life | www.laterlife.com |
| Wise Owls | www.wiseowls.co.uk |
| Forties People | www.fortiespeople.com |
| Directgov | www.direct.gov.uk |

## ✴ Resources for women returners

| | |
|---|---|
| Women Returners | www.women-returners.co.uk |
| Return 2 Work Mums | www.return2workmums.co.uk |
| Where Women Want to Work | www.wherewomenwanttowork.com |
| British Association of Women Entrepreneurs | www.bawe-uk.org |
| Women Like Us | www.womenlikeus.org.uk |
| Directgov | www.direct.gov.uk |

## ✴ Resources for people with disabilities

| | |
|---|---|
| Disabled Workers | www.disabledworkers.org.uk |
| Disability Job Site | www.disabilityjobsite.co.uk |
| Remploy | www.remploy.co.uk |
| Shaw Trust | www.shaw-trust.org.uk |
| Even Break | www.evenbreak.co.uk |

## ✴ Self-help resources

| | |
|---|---|
| NHS | www.nhs.uk |
| Self Help Directory | www.self-help.org.uk |
| British Association for Counselling and Psychotherapy | www.bacp.co.uk |
| British Psychological Society | www.bps.org.uk |
| Mental Health Foundation | www.mentalhealth.org.uk |
| Mind (Mental Health Charity) | www.mind.org.uk |
| Samaritans | www.samaritans.org.uk |
| Counselling Directory | www.counselling-directory.org.uk |
| Counselling Support | www.wpf.org.uk |
| International Stress Management Association | www.isma.org.uk |
| Depression UK | www.depressionuk.org |

| | |
|---|---|
| Depression Alliance | www.depressionalliance.org |
| Bipolar Organisation | www.mdf.org.uk |
| Alcoholics Anonymous | www.alcoholics-anonymous.org.uk |
| Gamblers Anonymous | www.gamblersanonymous.org.uk |
| Narcotics Anonymous | www.ukna.org |
| Beating Eating Disorders | www.b-eat.co.uk |
| Cruse Bereavement Care | www.cruse.org.uk |

## ✳ *Graduate career resources*

| | |
|---|---|
| Association of Graduate Careers Advisory Services | www.agcas.org.uk |
| Prospects: the official graduate careers website | www.prospects.ac.uk |
| European Graduate Career Guide | www.eurograduate.com |
| Directgov | www.direct.gov.uk |
| Grad Jobs | www.gradjobs.co.uk |
| Milkround job site | www.milkround.com |
| Graduate Jobs | www.graduate-jobs.com |
| Target Jobs | www.targetjobs.co.uk |
| Graduate Recruitment Bureau | www.grb.uk.com |
| The Big Choice: student and graduate jobs | www.thebigchoice.com |
| Graduate Career | www.graduatecareer.com |
| Inside Careers | www.insidecareers.co.uk |

## ✳ *Non-executive directorships*

| | |
|---|---|
| NED Exchange | www.nedexchange.co.uk |
| Non-Executive Directors Club | www.non-execs.com |
| First Flight Placements | www.nonexecutivedirector.co.uk |
| Executive Appointments | www.exec-appointments.com |
| Executives on the Web | www.executivesontheweb.com |

## ✳ *Consultancy/interim resources*

| | |
|---|---|
| Institute of Interim Management | www.iim.org.uk |
| Law Speed | www.lawspeed.com |
| Top Contract Consultant | www.top-contractconsultant.com |
| Contract Jobs | www.contractjobs.com |
| People 4 Business | www.people4business.com |

## ⚹ Career resources for moving to the UK

| | |
|---|---|
| Home Office | www.homeoffice.gov.uk |
| Graduate Study Options | www.graduatestudyoptions.com |
| UK Immigration Services | www.workpermit.com |
| UK Visa & Immigration | www.ukvisaandimmigration.co.uk |
| Directgov | www.direct.gov.uk |
| UK Council for International Student Affairs | www.ukcisa.org.uk |
| Migrate UK | www.migrate-uk.com |

## ⚹ Courses/skills development: academic/vocational/NVQs, etc.

| | |
|---|---|
| Learn Direct | www.learndirect.co.uk |
| Next Step | https://nextstep.direct.gov.uk |
| National Council for Work Experience | www.work-experience.org |
| Open University | www.open.ac.uk |
| Distance Learning Centre | www.distance-learning-centre.co.uk |
| UCAS | www.ucas.ac.uk |
| Hot Courses | www.hotcourses.com |
| NVQ courses | www.nvqcourse.co.uk |

## ⚹ Useful directories

| | |
|---|---|
| British Venture Capitalist Association | www.bvca.co.uk |
| Recruitment and Employment Confederation | www.rec.uk.com |
| Headhunters | www.headhuntersdirectory.com |
| Self Help | www.self-help.org.uk |
| Events/exhibitions | www.exhibitions.co.uk |

## ⚹ Self-employment resources

www.startups.co.uk
www.businesslink.org
www.chamberonline.co.uk
www.thebfa.org
www.inlandrevenue.gov.uk/startingup
www.homeworking.com
www.smallbusiness.co.uk
www.fsb.org.uk
www.companieshouse.gov.uk

✳ *Notes*

*(Continued)*

(Continued)

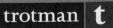

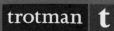